SMALL BUSINESS EXPERIENCE MARKETING

SMALL BUSINESS EXPERIENCE MARKETING

Building customer loyalty with memorable, high-impact, low-budget events

BRIDGET BAYER

BAMpdx | Independently published

Copyright © 2021 by Bridget Bayer. All rights reserved.

No part of this book may be reproduced or transmitted in any form or by any means, electronic, mechanical, photocopying, recording, or otherwise, without prior written permission of the publisher.

ISBN: 9798718958003

Library of Congress Control Number: TBA

Independently published.

Printed in the United States of America
First Edition

BAM (Business Association Management) | BAMpdx.com

For Kat, now that we are all grown up

ABOUT THE AUTHOR
Bridget Bayer

A serial entrepreneur, **Bridget Bayer** started her first business at age 13. Working primarily in hospitality, she eventually owned a successful café and catering business on a major main street in Portland, Oregon. Through planning countless small business promotional activities and gatherings, she developed a specialty in producing large and small events featuring memorable experiences. With a clientele that includes cities, Chambers, and Main Street associations, Bridget is an expert at building community through events.

Bridget Bayer's first book, **Street Fairs for Community and Profit,** is a how-to guide for creating signature events that turn ordinary Main Streets and small downtown areas into destination locations. The Street Fair guide instructs groups on how to strengthen their business community while reaching specific goals.

This book, **Small Business Experience Marketing,** is designed for individual business owners seeking to expand their marketing prowess. It is a straightforward manual of best practices focused on creating memorable experiences through sensory stimulation and community connections that provide long-term benefits to small business owners.

ACKNOWLEDGEMENTS

It's been a long road to completing this book, not least because creating community through experiences will never be done. I am especially thankful for the ideas, questions and willingness to share experiences from the many small business owners I encounter daily. We entrepreneurs are the lifeblood of every community. We take risks every day, primarily to make our businesses a success. Thank you for reaching towards long-term profitability and for all your efforts to better connect our world together.

First and foremost, I have to thank my darlin' husband, Peter Wilcox, for supporting me, in every way, while I practice being a professional writer. I am grateful for all the love and support that continues to come from family members, my chosen sisters, and fellow small business owners who remind me daily that they wish they had read this book when first opening their shops.

My most sincere thanks goes to my editor, Beck Luening, who started by chatting about the ideas in this book and ended by editing, proofing, formatting and making it a thousand times better. My favorite readers, Heidi Bayer, Sharon Drew Morgan, Nancy Chapin and Phillip Stanton, gave me critical feedback for which I am deeply indebted. Ira Pasternack is a superstar web guru who keeps my online presence real. Thank you to Jennie Komp, who helped me move along, and to Tex Thompson, author and teacher, who introduced us, but more importantly kept me laughing and learning from my mistakes.

Special recognition and appreciation goes to the many small business retail and service providers who helped provide insight into their masterpieces, sharing secrets of their successes and sometimes small disasters: Deborah Field, Paperjam Press; Emily, P's & Q's Market; Doppleganger Sarah Hart, Alma Chocolate; Heidi Johnson Bixby, Johnson Bixby WA Financial Planning; and Nancy Fedelem, Salty's Dog & Cat Shop. I am grateful to the Alberta Main Street staff and fellow volunteers who continue to lead the way in making their destination location equitable for all!

The Willamette Writers community continues to support me along with many other successful writers in the Pacific Northwest. A special thank you to Sarina Doyle who manages to make The Write Place, a weekly goal-oriented Zoom meeting, worthwhile and inspirational. Special kudos to Kate Ristau, successful young adult author, who unknowingly drives me with her delightful, cheery news and accomplishments! Likewise, Kathy Ware and all the Krewebies from the Mysti Krewe of Nimbus bring energetic diversions that energize and renew me with their creative enthusiasm.

I will never be able to thank my Mom enough. She instilled in me a powerful love for community, demonstrated by her actions that continue today well into her 80s. Plus, she taught me that "nobody's perfect." Also, I can't thank my brothers and sisters enough for showing me how to have fun while working and teaching me that the smallest detail can sometimes make the greatest impact.

AUTHOR'S NOTE

Pay special attention to the highlighted sections throughout this book offering valuable event-organizing tips from professionals, ideas for partnerships, and innovative ways to jumpstart your creativity.

> **PRO TIP:** A cadre of small business owners, professional marketers, caterers and event planners has reviewed this book and offer definitive suggestions for how professionals would operate under certain circumstances.

> **PARTNER OPP:** Partnering with other businesses on events contributes to the development of a strong, mutually suppportive business community over time. Sharing an activity and prompting cosponsors can make an event stronger, more interesting and more diverse.

> **FAST START:** Stop reading and start planning your own Experience Marketing event. Find inspiration not only in the practical ideas and suggestions offered in this book, but all around you: Take notes, record a voice memo, or snap a picture anytime you see something that sparks an idea for a memorable event experience.

QUICK REFERENCE:

PRO TIPS

Reuse decor and save	20
Shop clearance sales after holidays to save money	20
Do your cleaning early in the day	24
Use an event planning questionnaire to vet ideas brought by others	31
Consolidate your errands	36
Take advantage of online tools for free or low-cost design	58
Update promo videos to let people see event coming together	59
Embed code in announcement enabling one-click calendar addition	59

Use unique graphics or coupon codes to track marketing success. . . . 63
Make signs to encourage customers' self-expression 65
Set up a selfie station 65
Begin planning weeks in advance 70
Leave rented spaces as you found them. 75

PARTNER OPPS

Being a greeter or providing valet parking or coat check 19
Handling the arrangements for live entertainment. 21
Supplying refreshments 23
Providing SWAG, prizes or gifts with their logo 25
Reviewing plans for safety and liability issues (insurance agent) 34
"Task To-do" lists for partners 35
Reviewing contractor documents (attorney) 37
Lending plates, glasses, service-ware (neighborhood restaurant) 39
Assisting with promotion and public relations tasks 47
Collaborating as equal partners and sharing the credit. 57
Greeting, handling, and serving as a liaison for performers 70

FAST STARTS

Study ethnic restaurant practices for culture-specific experiences . . . 14
Example of classic pirate-themed event (sensory details) 23
Examples of off-beat/hybrid events (sensory details) 24
Planning Activity Part 1 32
Planning Activity Part 2 33
Experience Marketing ROI Exercise. 38
Example of being flexible and creative to stay within budget. 41
Maintain consistency to enhance your reputation 42
Partnership Exercise in 3 Parts. 48
Example of what is included in a complete event invitation. 59
Dress employees according to theme to set them apart 77

CONTENTS

About the Author vii

Acknowledgements ix

Author's Note: Quick Reference to Tips x

Introduction   Experience Marketing: An Overview 1

Chapter 1   Targeted Fun: Essentials Elements of Successful Experience Marketing 7

Chapter 2   Creating Memorable Events by Stimulating the Senses 13

Chapter 3   Planning and Evaluation Focused on More than Financial Returns 29

Chapter 4   Connecting to Partners and Building Community Relationships 45

Chapter 5   Promoting Events and Your Brand with Stimulating, Experiential Style 51

Chapter 6   Coordinating Experience Marketing Events Like a Pro. 69

Chapter 7   Closing Thoughts 81

Examples   Event Management Tools 83

Cargo Inc. entryway visually stimulates uplifting emotions, cueing guests' expectations upon arrival.

INTRODUCTION
Experience Marketing: An Overview

Imagine organizing fun activities involving everyone you know, plus people you want to know, as a way to build a long-term, prosperous business with deep customer loyalty. In essence, this is what Experience Marketing is all about—creating and "selling" experiences, not just products or services. Hosting experiential events that value a customer's time and attention gives them something a product alone cannot—a sense of community.

Experience Marketing uses events to interrupt the hamster-wheel of retail competition and found legacies of community cooperation. Connecting with people in this way demonstrates that you see them as more than a fleeting, hollow financial exchange, and is one of the foundation stones of building customer loyalty and trust. Whether you are a small business retailer or a professional service provider, forming long-term relationships with your customers is guaranteed to set your business apart from growing online competition.

Start with your strengths

You are an independent entrepreneur who has created a reliable job for yourself where you call the shots. You have little to no extra time to devote to marketing, let alone hosting special events, but you know you have a business worthy of attracting new customers and impressing the ones you have. You can guess that gaining customers might require steps into the unknown and possibly a steep learning curve. Assuredly, you will need the courage to fail.

This book shows you how to start small, teasing out intimate experiences at first, allowing you to make deeper, more sustaining connections via the one-on-one encounters that are an essential aspect of event production. As you gain confidence, Experience Marketing will boost your everyday sales and promotional activities with targeted, strategic use of sensory stimulation combined with the expanded community connections that bring deep, long-standing benefits to small business owners.

Identify what you don't know

Entrepreneurs are often restricted by what they already know. There is comfort in the familiar and if you're like me, you're too busy to realize that staying in your comfort zone may be what's holding you back. A first step in recognizing where you may need to push yourself is noticing where you procrastinate. Awareness of your own strengths and weaknesses—as well as your partners'—will be key when it comes to assigning roles during event organizing.

Modernize your methods

If you're reading this, then you are probably doing some kind of marketing and possibly realizing the same predictable results of sustaining, but not growing, your business. Have the courage to step outside of what is familiar. The original four Ps of marketing—Product, Place, Price and Promotion—are old and tired, though they are still taught in classes and relied on by some corporations. Worse, they are often anticipated by customers. The next generation Ps—Planning, Partnership, Promotion and Production—are the marketing strategies now being adopted by successful storefront retail and Main Street businesses.

Diversify your approach

Experience Marketing events are most successful when they anticipate and incorporate a variety of customs, habits and styles. Stuffier books would call this "diversifying your risk," but you will get further seeing this as "equitable collaboration." Involving more people doesn't just elevate the overall result, it works to create a community of people who share the same goals and the same investment in your mutual success.

Consider Small & Independent v. Big Box

No successful retailer markets their business the same way they did five years ago, or even one year ago. Before Covid-19, the proliferation of large retailers and online shopping had already overshadowed Main Street shopping. Big-box retailers have two major marketing advantages: blast-style advertising that expands in wide markets and pass-through supplier promotions. These unassailable marketing ploys drive customer acquisition and retention, as does the convenience of one-click sales and items drop-shipped within days, sometimes hours. Yes, it is undeniably easy to shop online, with the ability to compare prices, services, benefits and qualities. What's not to love?

People shop online to find specific items that are hard to find in local markets, but the fact is, there is limited joy in buying online. Among other things, online purchasing is impersonal and—beyond the satisfaction of acquisition—rarely offers the good feelings generated in human-to-human transactions. In contrast, face-to-face shopping experiences, especially in small, independently owned establishments, offer the warmth of a human interaction that just isn't possible in the machine world. Over time, these seemingly small face-to-face connections help build customer appreciation and loyalty, and ultimately, community.

Online orders can be fraught with technical glitches and errors. Merchandise misrepresentations or misconceptions are not uncommon. Buyers are manipulated with pictures of glamorous models. The picture that drew you in may not be what's actually in stock. Sizing can be frustrating too, when numbers don't match up to expectations, and there is no way to try things on before purchasing.

Poor craftsmanship, excess packaging and transportation costs are just a few of the downsides of mass consumption that overshadow the benefits of cost savings and convenience. Climate change is forcing consumers to consider the environmental costs of their buying habits, and global media is making it harder and harder to deny externalized effects such as human rights abuses of workers.

Equity concerns are also on many minds these days. Depending on your target market, closing this gap could be one of your niches—catering to those people who can't purchase online because they don't have safe, reliable internet access, a credit card, or even a home address. For these populations, small and local options are absolutely essential.

Join the movement to community

Even though online retail can be a gamble, it is on track to take down big-box stores, just as the big boxes diminished the business of Main Street retailers. With fewer and fewer retail options, shopping has simply become a chore, not much fun anymore, because it isn't the social experience that it used to be.

The good news is, as people tire of the experience retail has become, they will seek out the experience of Main Street retail shopping: that personal, one-on-one attention. This is one of the unique values a Main Street business can provide, and this book is about how to provide the best experiences possible. How to become irreplaceable to your customers by getting personal with them.

I'm talking about a level of genuine, insightful, customer service that elevates the buying experience while alleviating the anxiety that can come with new purchases. You can personally demonstrate to the buyer your honesty, integrity and knowledge. Best of all, you can learn these attributes by producing hands-on, personally focused, experiential events.

Main Street communities are lucky that the younger generation is showing a preference for community. They want the good energy that accompanies direct interactions with real people, eliminating foreign-based operators and corporate middlemen whenever possible. And small retailers can now offer the convenience of one-click shopping with more people using PayPal, Venmo, or flashing phones to make easy purchases.

Learn how to create truly memorable community events

Let's consider four common issues:

TOO COMPLICATED: Maybe you think that hosting an event is only for professionals. Just thinking about ordering food and scheduling musicians can put some people into an anxiety-filled tailspin. By the time you consider invitations, decorations, an extra marketing blitz, and collaborating with people you don't already know who may not share your level of investment, it's time to call 9-1-1.

> ***Good News:*** Experience Marketing events are not random acts conjured up and completed in a single week. They are orderly and well-planned promotional activities, with incremental goals that produce definable outcomes. Experience Marketing at its heart is sensory immersion. By stimulating and captivating customers, you will spark emotional reactions triggering feelings, ideas and memories that give a reason to pay attention. People will be incentivized to connect and retain loyalty more readily.

TOO EXPENSIVE: Some people hear Experience Marketing and their imagination is filled with the Hollywood image of big tents, lavish decorations and valet parking. Our imagination wears us down when thinking of customers entering through glistening storefronts, champagne and caviar in hand, complimenting the elaborate invitations and gossiping about the famous guest entertainment.

> ***Good News:*** Your Experience Marketing event doesn't have to compete with the Oscars after-party to be effective. You don't need lavish displays or name-dropping guest lists. Instead, the more relaxed you are, and the more you reach out to people on your level, without showing off, the more people will relax and enjoy the experience in a personal way. Partnering with other like-minded business owners, nonprofits, or even obscure connections will help to create remarkable, attention-grabbing events even at reduced costs.

TOO FRIENDLY: The world has told you that extroverts are the experts of party planning and you know you're not one. Inviting people to your home, even your business, terrifies you. You're an introvert, with a minimal social circle, probably filled with fellow introverts, so you don't know what to do first.

> *Good News:* In business, you have the opportunity to stage any activity your way, with no strings or family dynamics attached. You set the time that's right for you and your customer's lifestyle. You serve the kinds of refreshments you like. You choose the music or entertainment. That way, no matter what, you have an event you know you will enjoy. The mindset you bring to this effort affects every aspect of it, known as top-down modeling.

TOO UNFOCUSED: You've tried being a host before. You can't predict your results, so you end up breaking even and dissatisfied. Maybe you've been doing too much guesswork or tried too many things at once. You can't be sure which element worked and which one you might want to retire. You change your marketing approach each time, but the expenses grow with little return for your trouble.

> *Good News:* Focusing on specific target markets gain more than passing attention. Learning how they get their news, where they shop, read and play will educate even practiced marketers. That knowledge, coupled with distinct sensory input, will construct events that are less expensive with better results. Once you host an event, you will learn firsthand how to measure the benefits in new customers, increased exposure, more sales and increased community

This book demonstrates how to succeed at Experience Marketing by:

- Determining the kinds of experiences your customers are drawn to;
- Evaluating what you are doing to identify strengths and weaknesses of your current efforts;
- Setting accurate projections based on clear evaluations;
- Planning for specific outcomes;
- Using enhanced sensory focus to create memories;
- Recognizing opportunities to partner with others for mutual benefit, both short and long-term;
- Expanding outreach to attract more business while rewarding customer loyalty.

Experience Marketing events aim to please. Have plenty of helpers on hand to greet all attendees and serve your guests popular snacks and drinks to make them feel welcome.

CHAPTER 1
Targeted Fun: Essential Elements of Successful Experience Marketing

Experience Marketing Story #1: The Book Reading

A new author is looking for opportunities to publicize and sell her book. After reading about a local bookstore that has a book club meeting every month, she approaches the owner with an offer to do a book reading with book club members. She shows the bookstore owner her online author page, noting a good number of followers since the book's release. But the owner has never heard of the author and has her doubts. She looks over the flier from a reading the author held in a nearby town, but she's already made up her mind. She declines the offer, shaking her head sadly. "I lost my manager last summer and I just don't have the capacity to organize author readings. I don't even have time to host my own book club anymore." The author notices that although the store is bright and orderly, with engaging signs, it is empty of customers. It's early in the day, but the author can't help thinking that the memoir the owner reluctantly put down when she entered the shop seemed more important than their conversation. The author moves on to the next place on her list.

Investment: None!

Impact: None! The bookstore owner never seriously considered the opportunity. She probably knows little about the store's past promotional activities, since they were managed by someone else and were only for repeat customers. She never considered the possible benefits of an author reading, because she couldn't get past her doubts and her own deficits. The bookstore owner's skill was in displaying merchandise and point-of-sale marketing. She not only didn't know how to host events; she didn't know how to ask for help.

Experience Marketing Story #2: The Music Swap Meet

The owner of a new breakfast and lunch café notices a lull in customer traffic. The first rush, after grand opening, has tapered off to concerning levels. Not everyone who promised to come back has done so, but she knows people are always looking for something new. Opening was easy, but staying open would require ongoing creativity on her part. She checks in with her neighbor, the owner of a hair salon who has just started offering free Wi-Fi and the use of iPads for customers waiting for their up-dos and haircuts. The salon's afternoon hours barely overlap with the café's hours, so the two spend some time considering what their customers have in common, and how they can make the most of that overlap. Together they agree on a shared goal of reaching new customers.

It turns out that school-aged kids and their parents are a common denominator for both businesses. Their brainstorm session takes into account each business's different needs and their own abilities. They determine their best option is an after-school Music Swap Meet that includes a DJ and kid-friendly snacks with fun giveaways.

Both business owners shop for discounted snacks and drinks, and they combine their meager marketing budgets to print small fliers that they hand out to customers one month prior to the event. They also distribute fliers through the local schools and invest in a couple of ads on a local parent magazine website. The salon owner finds an up-and-coming DJ to curate the music and secures free downloads to use as giveaway prizes. The café owner pitches their collaboration to local newspapers and a radio station.

The Music Swap Meet focuses on good music, great service and generous treats. Both businesses are decorated with lively, colorful posters. Best of all, the two owners are on hand to meet and greet their customers face to face. Their event creates a memorable experience for all who attend, and both businesses see a substantial uptick in new customers for months afterward!

Shared Financial Investment: $400 each:

    $500   fliers and online ads
    $200   snacks and entertainment
    $100   giveaways

    $800   ($400 each)

Shared Time Investment: 11 hours each

    3 hours planning the event
  10 hours booking DJ, gathering refreshments, decorations and giveaways
    6 hours creating and buying ads, pitching to radio/newspaper
  <u>3 hours</u> printing and distributing fliers

  22 hours (11 hours each over 3 months)

Big Impact!

    28   "kids" scored free music after influencing their parents to attend
    40   parents and other adults attended
  120   email addresses collected to be used for future promotions and events
  650   clicks on a parent magazine website, securing a continuing partnership
  800   social media shares combined from the DJ, the parent magazine and both businesses

         + earned media: A local paper published an article and pictures

  22% increase in revenue from day of sales and returning customers that month

         + new crossover customers

Wouldn't you feel successful if you spent $400 and 11 hours and got that kind of return?

What's the difference between these two examples?

The Music Swap Meet focused on shared ideas and a collaborative approach to event marketing. The two business owners created a partnership that supported their individual goals while sharing the costs of producing an event. They intentionally set out to build community by asking for help and engaging other people in their promotion.

The Music Swap Meet was an immersive experience that included music geared to their target market, recognizable visuals and tasty snacks, thereby stimulating multiple senses and making memories for the customers—without significantly taxing the owners' resources. The more sensory experiences included, the greater potential an event has to be memorable.

The Book Reading was a nonstarter. Pitched by the author, the idea required the bookstore owner to do some work outside her skill set. The owner focused on the amount of work it might take without considering the possible payoff. Lack of experience, fear of promoting an author unknown to her, and a feeling of being overburdened kept her from recognizing the potential benefits of collaboration. Without a more detailed plan to present to the owner, she was unprepared to push past "No."

The author could have presented a more detailed plan for creating a memorable book reading. She could have prepared a list of potential partners that could be invited to evolve a simple book reading into an experience. She could have pitched a comprehensive plan that would stimulate sensory memories to strengthen customer loyalty. Developing an idea into an actual event requires people to get involved or it will have no chance of succeeding.

Ready for success? Read on...

Now more than ever, people are hungry for opportunities to connect with others. It is what makes us human. We naturally collaborate, even share a little bit of ourselves, when enjoying one another's company. Partnering with others improves our chances of success while sharing the risks of misadventure. We are also more likely to succeed when we carefully set goals, plan, then measure results.

This book is your guide for achieving Experience Marketing success. It explains how to build those collaborative partnerships. It details the process of planning Experience Marketing event promotions and shows you how to quantify results in order to increase your skill and success over time.

This book will empower you to move forward with confidence in planning and producing collaborative Experience Marketing events that work for your budget, fit within your time constraints and your lifestyle, and stimulate lasting memories and meaningful community connections for you and your customers.

Dress-up costume themes are an easy way to entice people's participation.

CHAPTER 2
Creating Memorable Events by Stimulating the Senses

An Experience Marketing event is, first and foremost, a thoughtfully crafted sensory experience. You are providing customers with something tangible, a narrative they can communicate to others. When done well, their emotions are triggered and they come away feeling transformed. The deeper the experiential immersion, the more memories are created, rewarding the customer for their time investment and strengthening their sense of loyalty to your business.

Restaurants have an inherent advantage in catering to people's basic needs. Customers arrive hungry, they are fed—usually well—and are transformed by the satiated feeling. In addition to taste and smell, the best dining experiences also engage our visual and auditory senses. Attentive service elevates the experience. Ethnic restaurants are embassies for their food's country of origin and provide built-in sensory experiences connected to their distinct culture. From the moment customers walk in the door, they partake in the traditional sights, sounds and smells of a place. Done well, they make dining with them a mini vacation, a fully immersive cultural experience.

> **FAST START:** For a one-time event, copy ethnic restaurant practices on a smaller scale. Promoting a new product from Holland? Adorn announcements with Dutch windmill cut-outs, serve gouda cheese and Stroopwafle cookies, and wear wooden shoes and orange clothing.

Successful Experience Marketing events are shaped by the sights, sounds, tastes, smells and feelings provided by you, the host. On a regular day, your business has a familiar ambience. When you create a special event promotion or activity, it should look and feel like a whole new scene. If you were hosting a special guest in your home, you would probably clean the house, carefully prepare some food, add flowers or decorations to the table, and set the mood with a favorite playlist. Similarly, every aspect of an Experience Marketing event needs to convey to customers or potential customers that we care about them and want them to enjoy the time they spend with us.

Many small business events are hampered by creative setting, or rather a lack thereof. Experience Marketing events are not the time for restraint. Budget permitting, you want to maximize whatever space you have and stretch your dollars into every possible nook and cranny. You can go wild and crazy with your decorations, as long as they're artful. Think home celebrations on steroids. The more color, flamboyance and expression you put into your promotions, the more your business will stand out and be remembered.

For inspiration, reflect on a memorable event from your past—one you created or attended. Examine all the elements that went into that experience with your mind's eye. What were the sounds, textures, food, features, specialty giveaways, door prizes, or live music that made it memorable for you? You will find that it is attention to details and multiple sensory elements that make events "pop."

Let your theme be your guide

The key to Experience Marketing events is having a clear vision and unwavering commitment to a chosen theme and ensuring all of the planned activities and visuals fit. If you have cool ideas that don't quite fit, save them for the next one, because the greatest impact comes from continuity of elements. You can choose themes that allow you to play up your strengths and downplay your weaknesses.

In executing theme-based events, strive to rouse all the senses, even the sixth sense, feelings, to make the strongest impressions. Sidewalk sales and open houses are two examples of classic marketing opportunities that have been staged by practically every retail business for generations. Even these boringly predictable sales can be transformed by focusing on emotional stimuli and incorporating creative themes.

Place-themed Experience Marketing events transport people to another place or time. Taking a cue from your products or services, transform your space into another place, taking the shopper out of the everyday. If the new product you are showcasing was made in England, the music might be British pop and feature English Bitter beer and chips. If your business caters to Spanish speakers, you will definitely want to serve *cerveza,* and maybe homemade tamales, while a Mariachi band serenades customers.

You can gear events to the age bracket of your target market and be socially conscious to boot. Staging kids' activities? Posters cheaply set the scene and environmentally friendly balloons that don't float away are a draw for both kids and their eco-conscious parents. For teens, project movie trailers, fun YouTube videos, or share inside secrets of musicians or sports stars at a "zero waste" event. For seniors, show enticing travel programs, host lecturers, play classic rock or Sinatra, or provide a reason for them to include their grandchildren.

Sometimes themes are suggested by a particular type of business. For example, an auto supply store might have a classic car parked out front, stimulating an emotional response while promoting their business. A children's dental office might have some big play "teeth" along with over-sized toothbrushes and tools kids can use to clean or fix them. Keeping continuity with these general themes makes sense for service businesses when hosting special events.

A theme can be as simple as "R&R." Give people a chance to kick back with a favorite beverage while shopping and invite a local maker, designer or service provider to engage with them in a relaxed and purposeful way. Show off a new accessory or clothing line at a comfortable bar or restaurant instead of your retail store.

Holiday themes

Business owners often think that to be noticed or to get their message to go viral, they must be 100% original. In a book titled *Originals: How Non-Conformists Move the World,* authors Adam Grant and Sheryl Sandberg prove through exhaustive research on current market trends that few people buy 100% original anything. In fact, average purchasing crazes demonstrate that consumers want things that are only a few steps away from the familiar. There is a sweet spot between what your customers know they want and what's new that might make them choose you over someone else.

Holiday themes are the most commonly utilized for event promos. People aren't intimidated by traditional holidays because attendees already know what to expect. But Christmas, Halloween, Valentine's Day and Independence Day events are so common, promotions will go unnoticed without your particular spin to make them memorable.

Think about how you already celebrate individual holidays. Can you add a twist that strikes a balance between the familiar and the new? Traditions from afar could be combined with local traditions. Tweaking the standard U.S. Holidays calendar by mixing promotions could lead to an alt-classic like a St. Patrick's Day Christmas Party or a Rocky Horror Valentine Show. Add a dash of plaid to traditional Valentines' decorations for National Boyfriends Day and display framed famous couples, feature favorite sports pros, and set up seating in pairs.

Planning for theme continuity

Below are five examples of easily recognizable holiday event promotions outlined with sensory components and other details that you can customize to fit with your personality and what works best for your business.

Before you start a brainstorming session, identify your audience. Knowing who you are designing an Experience Marketing event for is essential when it comes to choosing the sensory elements that will make it memorable.

The customizable details can reflect your particular world view while enhancing experiences for your audience. The sweet spot will depend partly on your specific target market, but it's not a fixed point, so pay attention when evaluating an event afterwards.

Holiday/Calendar Themes
[short list]

JANUARY: New Year, Carnival

FEBRUARY: Valentine's, Presidents Day

MARCH: Saint Patrick's, Spring Break

APRIL: Easter, Earth Day, Passover

MAY: Cinco de Mayo, Mother's Day

JUNE: Graduation, Father's Day

JULY: Independence Day, Summer

AUGUST: International Cats, Sisters' Day

SEPTEMBER: Labor Day, Rosh Hashanah

OCTOBER: Sweetest Day, Halloween

NOVEMBER: Election, Diwali, Thanksgiving

DECEMBER: Hanukkah, Christmas, Kwanzaa

Choral groups tug on heartstrings and bring authenticity to events.

16 SMALL BUSINESS EXPERIENCE MARKETING

Holiday Theme Sensory Detail Brainstorm Examples

Lunar New Year

Colors: Red, gold, yellow, green
Decorations: Chinese or Asian décor, Zodiac, spring, new moon, families
Music: Instrumental, songbirds
Food: Sticky cake, dumplings, seafood, cookies, tea, sake
Activity: Seed kits, wishing trees, 5 elements—metal, water, wood, fire, earth
Entertainment: Fireworks, parades, visiting, family photo booth, shrines
Special Offering: Red envelopes with discount coupons or coins
VIP Customers: "Honor" symbol (button, badge, cords)
Collaboration: Partner with authentic Asian businesses

Kids' Valentine ABCs—Always Better with Chocolate

Colors: Red, pink, chocolate brown
Decorations: Hearts, letters of the alphabet (A, B, C), chocolate
Music: Guitar singer, love songs, Sesame Street, Elvis
Food: Desserts and candies
Activity: Card-making station, colored paper, scissors, stickers, karaoke
Entertainment: Puppeteer, magician, face-painter, costumed characters
Special Offering: Social media screen where people can display songs, art, and poetry
VIP Customers: Special valentines
Collaboration: Invite schools, art/craft stores; music, dance and theater studios

Saint Patrick's—Lucky Day

Colors: Green, gold
Decorations: Four-leaf clovers, Celtic knots, spring flowers
Music: Folk, comedy, Irish dancing
Food: Gold foil-wrapped chocolate coins, green mints
Activity: Color-able clovers, stickers, find discounts at the end of rainbows
Entertainment: Irish dancers, live band, children's storytellers, Leprechaun
Special Offering: "Lucky Clover" coupon good until the next Saint's Day
VIP Customers: Special discounts; collector items rare for your business
Collaboration: Feature products from jewelers, gift shops and restaurants

4th of July—National Parks

Colors: Red, white, blue
Decorations: Parks and nature posters, parks projections, state flags, vacation photos, live nature cams
Music: Brass or marching band, acoustic singer-songwriter, nature sounds
Food: Camping foods, s'mores, popsicles, refillable water station
Activity: Flag making, scavenger hunt, view finders, match photo games
Entertainment: Wild animal coloring pages; wildflower, tree or bird ID game; state puzzles
Special Offering: Personalized park flags, park passes
VIP Customers: Vintage camping, picnic or cooler items, VIP seating
Collaboration: Partner with existing fireworks display/parades for VIP seating

Halloween—Ghosts of the Past

Colors: White, gray, black, blood red
Decorations: Cobwebs, spiders, ghosts, black lights, haunted mansion backdrop
Music: Spooky organ music, classical dirges
Food: Vampire wine, Dead Guy Ale, hot cider, chocolate
Activity: Face-painted ghosts, video selfie "ghosts" with special lighting effects
Entertainment: Actors and authors tell or read ghost stories
Special Offering: Selfie station photo booth with scary clothes and props
VIP Customers: Horror movie or haunted house tickets
Collaboration: Local costume or retail store discounts, haunted house tickets

Experience Marketing involves *all* the senses

A successful Experience Marketing event eases shoppers' anxieties with uplifting visual, aural, olfactory and tactile stimuli. In other words, fears around decision-making and budget will soon fade in a fun atmosphere where their senses are tickled with delightful sights, smells and sounds.

The good feelings start at your front door when you greet people in person, or when they see the lively, colorful signs directing them to the good stuff—anything from chair massages to cocktails or mocktails. Relax and chat with customers as if they came just to see you. (Maybe they did!) Adorn shoppers with colorful bead necklaces, flowers for their hair, or Hawaiian leis. Let them hear the ocean and feel the salt spray. In other words, to turn a regular sale or promotion into something truly special, catering to all the senses.

THE HUMAN TOUCH

People are what make Experience Marketing events possible, and people are always the most important part. You, and by extension, your business, will be remembered when you make an effort to connect with the people who attend.

Greeting people personally and remembering them by name makes them feel welcome and valued. This old-fashioned version of customer service is making a comeback! People will step up to be a customer when you make eye contact, smile, ask what they are looking for—when you see and treat them as an individual. This is a special area where you can differentiate your business. It seems obvious; but if you go out of your way to do your best for people, they will appreciate it and want to reciprocate.

If you, the host, are a diehard introvert, you can promote a trusted manager or employee to be your primary customer ambassador. Just be aware that if, or when, they no longer work for you, it may hurt your business. You may also hire a coordinator or greeter for your event, but unless they are a recognizable face and/or knowledgeable about your business, they won't be as effective.

It's normal for people to come together for food, music and shared activities. If you invite people, make them feel welcome, provide an entertaining environment, and genuinely make an effort to get to know them; then most people, even customers, will feel relaxed and be receptive to you and your message. You don't need to pretend to be what you're not. Don't gush about your insecurities, but don't keep them all inside either. Nothing makes us more relatable and connects us to others like admitting we're human, but hopeful.

> **PARTNER OPP:** Ask a partner to be a greeter, or offer valet parking or coat check service for a touch of class.

SIGHT

Decorations are the first thing people see upon entering a space. You want your business to look and feel different for the event duration. The best decoration is you and your employees dressed in costume or on theme for the occasion. Wear a cloak, tiara, face make-up, or a special t-shirt to signal the difference in your business that day.

Keep your target market in mind when considering visual displays and decor. Set up or rearrange your store to show off what you want people to notice or be drawn in by. Hanging sale signs at belly-button level makes them easy to find without dominating.

Color sets the mood. Create fun, frivolous ambience with bright primary and secondary colors. For bold looks, stick to 1–3 high-contrast colors like white and red, or blue and yellow. For more serious events, use soft, muted colors. Use black and silver to convey elegance. For comfort, use strong jewel tones. Use warm colors for a sense of adventure.

Remember your brand. Even for a one-day promotion, stick with colors, shapes or other design elements reminiscent of your existing marketing brand.

For very special occasions, use real tablecloths, china, silver and glassware, and hire a professional catering crew. Print name cards, programs and menus, customizing for greater effect—remember to add color!

Lighting not only illuminates, but it can also evoke excitement, relaxation, energy—a whole range of emotions depending on the color, lumens and type of fixture. Adjust your lighting (with attention to safety) to change the vibe. Change the color by using different colored lightbulbs or by lining glass shades with colored tissue paper, keeping in mind that lighting is all about mood. Changing color can also change expectations.

Candles inside glass vases or glass bricks are a safe way to add low light, creating an air of mystery or romance. Open flames are a bad idea in any crowded environment, however, and LED candles make a good replacement. Dimmable lights are a good choice whenever possible; with today's "smart" technology, some lightbulbs can be remote controlled and put on a timer.

For special effects, use a small projector to sprinkle stars on your ceiling, or project spooky branches, ghosts, or a snowstorm on your indoor walls. Summer fiestas and wintertime celebrations both benefit from twinkle lights or paper lanterns, strung strategically, indoors or out.

> **PRO TIP:** Reuse decor and save!
>
> - If you have a place to store decorations or thematic props, you will save time and money in the long run by reusing and re-purposing festive décor.
> - Use real red tablecloths for the holiday season, then reuse for Valentine's Day and again for Fourth of July festivities, adding blue and white pieces.
> - Fill the same clear vases with different colored plastics, stones, or beads. Use silk flowers instead of buying fresh, depending on your target market.
> - Most fall decorations can easily be adapted from harvest, to Halloween, to Thanksgiving, changing combinations and color focal points like red apples for harvest, orange squashes for Halloween, golden corn for Thanksgiving.
> - Don't be afraid to break out the spray paint to upcycle or repurpose items again and again. You can give new life to old or cheap candleholders with sparkly metallic paint.
> - Black lights purchased for Halloween can also work well for adult birthdays or anniversaries, Back to School and Father's Day events.
>
> **PRO TIP:** Shop clearance sales after each holiday to save money.

SOUND

Have you ever had the urge to dance while shopping the aisles of a store blasting a good soundtrack? One of the easiest ways to transform an event into a memorable experience is to stimulate the brains of your target audience with music or sound. Endorphins are stimulated when we hear sounds we recognize. The age range of your target market is an important consideration, along with theme, in choosing music.

Sound can be featured front and center or eased into the background of your space. (If the music is loud, direct your attendees, with signs or verbally, to quieter places where they can chat if they wish.)

Recorded Music is an easy way to provide powerful emotional stimulus. Don't just put on the radio. Create a custom soundtrack, knowing that music sets the mood:

- Classical = elegant, romantic
- Jazz = familiar, improvised, hip, relaxed
- Hip hop / rap = edgy, rebellious, the good life
- Acoustic, alternative rock = cerebral, formal or folksy, emotional
- Classic rock, pop, country = families, fun
- Current Top 20 hits = new, forward thinking, active

Live Music makes a space even more vibrant and stimulating and it's worth your investment when you see tired shoppers being reenergized and feeling grateful. Often, you can find local singer-songwriters who will perform for free or low cost (with a tip jar) in exchange for publicity. Other entertainers may be willing to barter for products or services. Don't just offer them a chance to perform; promote them by offering to sell their CDs and include their names on your advertising and signage. Have fun finding performers by checking them out live before any scheduling takes place.

Buskers—street performers such as living statues, puppeteers, magicians, unconventional instrument musicians, character artists, or fortune tellers—are also great options for featured entertainment. Buskers can be clowns designing balloon hats, making music from a variety of instruments, doing face painting, juggling or acrobatics. They can be great at entertaining people who have to wait in lines. Again, offer buskers more than just exposure; they need to make a living too.

> **PARTNER OPP:** Giving a partner the opportunity to recruit, schedule and pay for performers can be a great way to afford a spectacular entertainer who will deliver a truly memorable experience.

Special Effects can be considered as your budget allows. Most small business owners lack the time and skills necessary to put on an elaborate, large-scale or upscale event. The bigger it gets, the greater the need to hire experienced people to make it go smoothly. When you are ready, consider hiring professional sound, lighting, staging, entertainment and special effects crews. Experienced caterers add effects by dressing servers according to themes. They may also add lighting, wall and table decorations. However, do not leave everything to the professionals. You or your coordinator will want to be there from beginning to end to make certain the theme and intent is not forgotten or diluted down to an ordinary, forgettable event.

TASTE

Refreshments both draw people in and entice them to stick around. People may come for the promised experience, but they will stay for the food. When you don't feed people, they may stay for an hour. If you feed them and have entertainment, you can expect them to stay as long as 2 or 3 hours.

Warm soups, stews and roasted nuts remind people of harvest and winter; cold gazpacho, watermelon and popsicles, of summer—no matter what time of year it is. Impart a feeling of the lazy days of summer in January with BBQs and fresh vegetables, or celebrate Christmas in July with candy canes and wrapped packages used as "trays" for food displays.

Whether or not you have the space for a large serving area, refreshments are mandatory for Experience Marketing events. Providing a sample of locally made chocolates, cheeses, jams, or just about anything will be appreciated by shoppers. Food tastings are a great way to put people in a frame of mind to try new things:

- Tomatoes, apples, pears, squash—sample a range of flavors in different varieties
- Wines, cheeses, chocolates—always a draw
- Pet treats for four-footed friends

Beverages are an integral part of the taste experience. Infuse a fresh water dispenser with slices of lemon, cucumber or watermelon rind. Invoke seasonal moods and memories by offering your guests cinnamon-spiced drinks or iced drinks in coolers.

Get the most out of food-centric events by enticing people with new or unusual beverages and pairing combinations:

- Wine paired with cheese, bread, picnic fare, appetizers
- Local craft ciders, distilled spirits, new cocktails
- Beer paired with nuts, salty snacks, chocolate, veggies
- Root beer, ginger ale, or other non-alcoholic drinks paired with kids' snacks

Offer small samples, especially if alcohol is involved, and follow strict liquor licensing rules. Having festooned bartenders on hand preparing delicious drinks, with alcohol or without, can transport people out of the everyday, with professional service imparting a sense of high value.

> **PARTNER OPP:** Asking partners to supply refreshments is an easy way to grow your business community.

While not always easy to pull off well, display counts a lot when serving food, because "we eat with our eyes first." Add tasteful decorations whenever possible to complement your branding. Using glass instead of plastic is a classy touch, if you have the storage and budget.

Arrangements can enhance your theme. Set drinks out in a Christmas tree pattern, stack food so it looks like your logo. When preparing your platters, think about what could make an ordinary cheese and cracker spread look like it is part of your theme.

> **FAST START:** For a classic pirate theme, use skull-and-crossbones tablecloths and treasure-map napkins. Give away pieces-of-eight gold coin treats. Offer "a bottle of rum," as refreshment—either non-alcoholic or the real thing.

SMELL

Smell is the most underutilized sensory stimulus, for good reason. The same aroma may mean different things to different people. While this is the case for all of the sensual stimuli that go into an Experience Marketing event, scent has the potential to awaken deep-seated memories, so it's wise to go sparingly, allowing aromas to enhance, not to dominate it. Let your theme guide you in choosing the right aromatic touch.

Automated air fresheners can work magic to spark the senses. Lavender is relaxing, ginger is stimulating, and roses not only smell good but are gorgeous to admire. Fresh air is always popular for springtime and summer events.

Scented candles used in your lighting scheme can add holiday ambience, springtime breezes, or a spa experience.

Food and drink aromas add a vibe even if people aren't eating. Coffee reminds people of morning, cinnamon or nutmeg of the holidays, popcorn of movies, lemon of cleanliness, to name a few.

Aromatherapy diffusers release essential oil scents into the air to energize, relax, or help ease anxiety. Essential oil samples (a dab on the wrist for example) can be offered to customers as a personal aromatic. These oils are strong and best used in small doses.

> **PRO TIP:** Stark, stringent cleaners tend to be offensive to the nose, so do your cleaning early in the day before any guests arrive.

FEELINGS

Create ambience with thoughtful planning. Take the time to define the mood you want to create, then set about arranging your physical environment and adding the sensory elements that will best evoke that mood. Think about your target market: How will they use your product or service? What experience will make them feel comfortable yet enlivened? Try to give them that experience in your store.

Captivate people as they walk through the door with climate control. Crank up the heat and turn on the fans to simulate warm ocean breezes. Add a wave soundtrack and you've set the stage for a summer beach party.

Furry, fluffy plush toys or displays can evoke warm and fuzzy feelings. Similarly, a "Yule log" picture on a large-screen TV or computer monitor can evoke an old-time holiday mood, adding a sense of warmth to a large room. Turn up the heat—literally—to warm and relax people. If the room feels hot and stuffy, open windows or doors and use fans to circulate the air.

Experience Marketing events often incorporate different zones for different purposes. A clearly visible kids' space can turn shoppers into buyers because it allows them time to make selections while momentarily freed of the distraction of children. A lounging space created with grouped seating or bar stools at high-top tables provides a resting place for partners who might otherwise pull the potential shopper away. Arrange seating in clusters to encourage visiting, in rows for learning, or around tables for eating.

> **FAST START:** Celebrate Christmas in July! Crank up the AC to simulate cold weather. Wear winter gear. Offer blankets and warm beverages. Play holiday music.
>
> Turn your sleepy office into sci-fi fun for Techies Day by piling gently used electronics on a table with wire and glue to invite robot creations. Arrange loose wires, artfully displayed, in a vase for a centerpiece. Project sci-fi films on monitors. Invite robotics students to demo their inventions.

Evoke joy with giveaways. Thoughtful giveaways are things people recognize as treats. Anything that pampers the body and makes them feel good will work. Consider giving away seasonal product samples, like hand sanitizer or sunscreen. Never underestimate a branded bag. They turn every customer into a walking billboard and can be customized on a budget. The more unexpected and delightful your giveaways, the more attendees will remember you.

SWAG (Stuff We All Get) is a great way to stand out from the crowd. Just remember that *no* SWAG is better than cheap, off-theme, or inappropriate SWAG. Start small.

Standard SWAG includes water bottles, keychains, lotions, pencils and pens, bookmarks, magnets, pins and buttons. Experienced Marketing–based SWAG ideas include:

- **Souvenir pictures:** Today's photo booths offer the capability of uploading pictures to social media sites and emailing pictures to guests. Pictures can also be added to items like magnet frames, plaques, ribbons, ornaments and snow globes.

- **Collectors' items:** Event-specific and branded medallions, hats, ties, t-shirts, socks, scarves, umbrellas, mugs, wine glasses, shot glasses, ornaments, towels, toothbrushes, bumper stickers, temporary tattoos, specialty prints and feet or hand warmers.

- **Edible treats:** Sweets, savories, beverages or anything goes here, but try to always have both salty and sweet options to maximize sales. (If you already sell salty snacks, give away sweets, if you already sell sweets, give away salty snacks.)

- **Selfie station with props and SWAG:** In addition to a decorated area, offer thematic props to enhance the experience for people capturing their own photos. Reward those who post pictures with your hashtag, preferably with a fun SWAG item they get to keep.

> **PARTNER OPP:** Partners love to provide SWAG and things that have text or a logo on it that reminds users of their brand. Invite suppliers and vendors to partner by donating door prizes, samples or small gifts. Allowing them to include their logo gives them the opportunity to reach customers too.

Build Brand Loyalty by incorporating any of the following elements in your Experience Marketing events.

Coupons: If you plan to hand out a coupon or event flier, clearly state a "Call to Action" that invites them back, or prompts them to sign up online or follow a link—something that will connect them to you and others. Don't forget an "use by" date and include a code to better track your return on investment. (*More on ROI in Chapter 5.*)

Contests: Let guests win prizes by counting popcorn in a pumpkin, or computer bits on a chip, anything that engages their brain, then their fingers when they register their vote. Carnival game nostalgia works well for older markets like Baby Boomers, but counting the number of squares on a space shuttle panel will attract millennials as well. Know your target market!

VIP Rewards: Recognize "regulars" or repeat customers with access to special seating areas, commemorative pins or stickers signifying VIP status. Have a greeter at the door ready to snap a picture of them holding a gilded empty frame up to their face with a VIP label. Post only the best photos to encourage loyalty and attract others to join.

An alternative to honoring preselected VIPs is to ask customers to complete a survey to gain VIP access. Classic loyalty programs reward repeat customers with free stuff or discounts after so many purchases. Go further and use nametags, VIP buttons, or ribbons to signify their special status. This tactic works very well for service businesses, business-to-business (B2B) meetups and professional groups.

Making space at partner planning meetings to hear a diversity of opinions will increase creativity and help build an event that strengthens customer bases.

CHAPTER 3

Planning and Evaluation Focused on More than Financial Returns

Planning an Experience Marketing event begins with answering a few key questions to clarify your goals and priorities. The first question is "Why?" Being clear on the rewards you are after will help you push through the obstacles that inevitably arise.

All actions begin with thoughts, so your first step is to get your ideas out of your brain and onto the page. It's funny how many ideas seem great until we outline them. Others seem ho-hum until they are described, and then they come to life.

Don't judge your ideas until you have outlined them using the following event planning questionnaire.

EVENT PLANNING QUESTIONNAIRE

Answering these questions will give you an outline for your event. You don't have to answer all the questions in one sitting. Write down what you can and add more thoughts as they come to you. Consider multiple ideas with multiple questionnaires if you want. When based on a clear and honest beginning assessment, imagining and planning Experience Marketing events can be great fun.

GOALS: Why have an event?

- What are your realistic immediate, mid-range and long-term goals?
- What are your return on investment (ROI) goals?
- What are your "impossible dream" goals for the event?

BENEFIT: What will you get out of it?

- How will the event benefit you, your business, brand or partners?
- How will your customers benefit?

AUDIENCE: Who do you expect to come to the event and why?

- Who is your target market (TM)?
- Who else might participate?
- Who else would you like to invite, or wish would come? (leave room to dream)

THEME: What is the event all about?

- What themes are already present in your business?
- What have your customers been talking about or asking for?
- What is in the public eye or current zeitgeist?
- What seasonal holiday are you wanting to celebrate?
- What will you call the event?

TIMING: When is the best time for the event?

- In what month or season would you like it to take place?
- What time of day will it be scheduled—morning, afternoon or evening? (Work out a time range.)
- Is this an annual or a one-off event?

SETTING: Where will the event take place?

- Where is the location? Is it indoor or outdoor, online or a combination?
- Are there any costs involved in securing the space?
- How do you imagine the setting will look and feel to guests?
- What kind of sensory experiences can be added at this site?
- Will the event require tables? chairs? shade tents? porta-potties?

ACTIVITIES: What will happen at the event?

- What does your TM generally like to see, hear, taste or appreciate?
- What sensory experiences will be memorable and resonate with your TM?
- What fits your theme?

PROMOTION: How will you create a "buzz" about your event?

- What marketing tools do you already have in place that could be used to promote it?
- Who among your partners and business community might promote it?
- What is your advertising budget?

FUNDING: How can you make an event budget that is NET positive over time?

- What might partners contribute to participate?
- What financial impact will it have on your business?

PARTNERS: Who among your business associates might support the event while benefitting from your ideas and leadership?

- Is there synergy with like-minded businesses or community groups?
- Will people or businesses donate items for games and/or raffle items?
- How can you leverage the event to build stronger partnerships?

MISSION: What level of success is needed to satisfy your goals?

- What outcome(s) do you need to see, to make it worth the effort?
- What would make it worth repeating and improving?

EXIT STRATEGY: What do you stand to lose if you decide to cancel?

- What is your point of no return?
- What are your back-up plans in case you, your staff or partners are unable to attend?
- How will you communicate a cancellation in a way that doesn't hurt your business?

> **PRO TIP:** Imagine the bookstore owner in our first example. What if, instead of turning away the author wanting to do a book reading, the owner asked them to complete a similar questionnaire? When approached with an unfamiliar idea, invite the person making the proposal to outline their vision more completely and provide a clearer path to action.

Planning and Evaluation Focused on More than Financial Returns

> **FAST START: Planning Activity Part 1**
>
> Write down some possible activities that might work in your business. Think about what your customers might think is fun, extremely elegant, or wacky, anything that could really stimulate their senses.
>
> Narrow your list down to the three ideas that get you the most excited and would be the easiest to host within the next three or four months.
>
> Make a list of what you already have (connections, partners, props, decorations, marketing channels, etc.) and people you already know that you'd be comfortable working with in some capacity (vendors, other business owners, club or community members).

Practice R&D

Not sure where to start? Practice a little R&D (Rip-off and Duplicate).

Check out the promotional events around you. Consider whether any of the winning ideas that catch your attention can be scaled, up or down, to fit your business. Keep in mind your target market when researching examples. When you find an event you'd like to emulate, ask your staff, friends and customers what they like or dislike about them. Take their answers into consideration when answering your planning questions. Bouncing ideas off others will eliminate guesswork, minimize your risk, and give you newfound confidence.

Small Investment	Big Impact
Search online using keywords that people would use to find your business. Research how like-business promos are structured.	Replicate their live or online promotions. Tailor successful advertising and sales techniques to your own business.
Copy a promotional event, adapting it to fit your business size and scope, then add experiential activities.	Save time figuring out themes, activities and places to promote by using what works for similar businesses as a template.

> **FAST START: Planning Activity Part 2**
>
> Review your listed activities from Part 1, then answer all the remaining questions on the questionnaire. Your answers don't have to be exact yet; just outline the idea.
>
> Follow through by researching real costs by the end of the week. Solicit quotes for ads, rentals, decorations. Even the tightest schedules can accommodate researching one or two budget items or vendor questions each day.
>
> If an idea stands out as a real possibility after this initial research, make time within the next week to sit down and complete a detailed draft using the event planning questionnaire.

Budget money

Here are the most common budget considerations you will face when planning events:

- How much money do you typically spend on marketing and promotion annually?
- Are you able to dedicate specific funds for event marketing?
- How much can you budget for one event?
- What is the cost of participation in a larger event?
- What are your projected short-term or long-term gains?

Many tech assistance advisors, including SCORE (Service Corps Of Retired Executives), suggest allocating about 10% of your annual budget to marketing. In a new market, it could easily be double. You get to decide what type of marketing to include in your budget. Make informed, profitable decisions by calculating your ROI from past events, point-of-sale merchandise displays, or plain old advertisements. In planning for long-term growth and sustainability, a lot depends on your target market, as is the case in most business decisions.

Your planning outline will generate a list of tasks for you to follow as well as the beginnings of an itemized list of expenses for your budget. The outline will also be an indispensable tool when you decide to put your plan into action. Continue to update your planning outline as you gain new ideas, new partners, or new opportunities.

Insurance: One part of keeping an Experience Marketing event on budget is having insurance in place that protects you from unforeseen expenses. Check with your insurance provider to see if special events are covered under your normal policy, and if so, to what extent. If separate or additional insurance is needed, don't hesitate to add an additional certificate of liability for partners, use of property and borrowed items.

> **PARTNER OPP:** Ask your insurance agent to partner with you by reviewing safety and other plans. Promote their business in return.

Budget time

Experience Marketing event organizing, like any other skill, is learned through practice. You will get quicker and better at it each time you do it. If this is all new to you, give yourself permission to go through a learning phase, and trust that if you keep at it you will develop the skills to make it a natural extension of your business acumen.

Time needs to be considered when planning your budget, not just money. Think about how much personal time you can afford to invest. (*See Timeline and Task List Examples at the end of this book.*) Calculate how much time specific tasks will take and plan to spread the work out over a couple of months. Ordering one centerpiece will only take about 15 minutes, but ordering floral displays for a stage or focal point will involve reviewing multiple options and layouts. Think about how much time you can budget to get started; then figure out how much can be contributed by employees and potential partners.

Once you have zeroed in on an ideal date—one that works for you and your target market —you can plot out the timeline. List-maker apps, standard event planning apps like Clickup, Asana, Mobilize and project management software or linked worksheets can all be used for keeping track of tasks over time. Use one that you can afford and feel comfortable using. Check the BAMpdx.com website for current recommendations and reviews of online resources for event management. Space out specific tasks, using a regular calendar or online task management tool to keep track. Think about whether any of your tasks have sub-tasks to itemize and track. List out all details as specifically as possible.

Task & To-Do lists

Four months is enough time to plan, stage and produce a small Experience Marketing event all by yourself. That's four months from the day you decide to do it to the actual day of the event. If you are including other business partners, you'll need to be respectful of their time, so plan on bringing them onboard at least six weeks before the event. Set a goal to have everything done one week early. That way, you will either be well rested, or you will have extra time to problem-solve last-minute glitches.

When partnering, make clear notes about who is tasked with research, communications, coordination and production of specific activities. Task assignments are more easily fulfilled when worked into the daily routine of everyone involved in organizing. A shared calendar, posted online or wherever people are most likely to see it, works great as a reminder and for accountability. Being able to provide a well-organized task list with sub lists outlining all responsibilities and expectations for getting tasks done makes it easier to enlist partners' participation.

Example: A to-do list for ordering flowers might contain all these sub tasks, with columns for noting who is responsible and expected completion date/time beside each task:

- Decide what to order.
- Choose a floral vendor (and backup in case of a problem).
- Determine payment arrangements.
- Place the order.
- Arrange for pickup or delivery.
- If delivery, schedule date and time.
- Make the payment.
- Make confirmation call the day before delivery.
- Serve as contact and be on hand to receive the flowers when delivered.
- Take responsibility for flower display.

> **PARTNER OPP:** A great way to enlist partners is to have a "task to-do list" ready to go that outlines everything necessary to complete a task so they can: (a) know that you are thoughtful and organized; (b) know what is expected (don't have to reinvent the wheel); and (c) have a high potential for success.

Plan, then market

Event planning can feel as overwhelming as trying to eat an elephant. As the joke instructs, just do it one bite at a time. The detailed planning process allows you to spread out your task to-do lists over a manageable period of time. If the planning stage feels overwhelming, break that up into smaller pieces. Treat your planning as "Part 1" of organizing an Experience Marketing event and marketing of the event as "Part 2." Doing a little something each day, instead of everything the day before, will ensure a more successful event as well as a more enjoyable process.

Delegate wisely

When delegating tasks, the question is not who is willing to manage information, money, or promotional tasks, but who will manage them well? Some tasks can easily be delegated to someone else. Hate bookkeeping? Delegate budgeting and expense-tracking to an accountant or finance person. Hate social media? Ask a student who's looking to build their portfolio or resume. Never get around to writing thank-you notes? Ask a partner to send thanks. People who take pleasure in certain tasks may bring an artistic touch you wouldn't have considered.

> **PRO TIP:** Save time by picking up extra items in advance when you are out doing errands, making bank trips, or on the way to and from work.

Digital delegation

While online shopping isn't always a good thing, it can make event coordination easier, but only if you start early. Search for special promotional items online and take good notes while searching. Collect screen shots, note dates, times, contact information, and website URLs from sites you may want to revisit, and create folders, both physical and online, to keep track of these items. Also, save emails, web orders and as much detail as possible from online resources you have utilized in the past.

Consider hiring professionals

You likely can't afford to contract professionals for all the tasks needed, but if you can outsource what you don't know, you can focus instead on what you do best. You probably know what you are good at by now, but in case you need reassurance, take an online Meyers Briggs test, learn from enneagrams, or take a free psychological test like those available at *123test.com*. Even more important than knowing what you excel at is understanding where you lack expertise.

A contractor may be able to help you by dealing with minute tasks, enabling you to stay focused on your larger goals. Contracting involves money, of course; if you are on a budget, you might look into online human services like Fiver.com or TaskRabbit.com to get tasks done cheaply.

When relying on others, even professionals, build in time to provide clear instructions and sufficient oversight, including correction if necessary. Contractors need direction and clear guidelines, especially the first time they work with you.

Even if you hire a friend, insist on a contract, or a specific, detailed agreement, so that everyone knows who is doing what, when and how. Write a clear list of duties and agreed-upon expectations, contingencies and reimbursement schedule. Note every time approval is needed. If the first contractor you hire doesn't match your expectations, don't hesitate to try someone else next time.

Eventually, an event may get so popular that you will need to contract with a production company or an individual contractor to coordinate activities. As you grow your business, keep a firm eye on your goals while developing partnerships to grow a deep-rooted community.

> **PARTNER OPP:** Consider getting a legal review of any document prepared by a contractor by offering the attorney promo space on invitations and fliers in exchange for their professional services. This might be an opportunity to build community with a partner not normally engaged in events.

Evaluation

Measuring your results will reveal the pot of gold at the end of your Experience Marketing event rainbow. Do this evaluation any way you like—in writing, with a voice recorder, or even a video—but don't skip it. The information you gain will help you recognize trends and shorten your learning curve for producing successful events in the future.

Commit to tabulating results immediately after each Experience Marketing event. Prepare a checklist to record information before, during and after. Start wherever you are, even if it's at the end of the night on the back of a napkin. Take full account of your successes and don't forget the weak points. Be honest about what worked best and what didn't work.

A full post-event evaluation should be done within the week. An objective assessment will provide you invaluable data for future planning. If you're going to go through all the effort of producing an event, it is essential that you value a clear accounting of your results as highly as you do the financial returns it may provide.

There isn't a single way to evaluate events, but I recommend starting with that list of goals you set initially. Mark the goals that you hit; that's your general overview. Next, dive into the numbers, with an accountant if necessary. Evaluate on your own, too, because accountants don't normally quantify soft returns like the strength of new partnerships. Take note of your own time, expenditures, sales numbers and attendance. Look at your overall results and then factor in returns such as elevation of your reputation and respect in the community.

Evaluation analysis teaches you to work smarter, not harder, so you can be more relaxed and confident the next time.

Evaluation metrics

Your Experience Marketing event evaluation is like a report card. Using metrics to evaluate results provides solid information on which to base future events. Your evaluation might track:

- Statistics for your specific goals
- Numbers of people who attended, watched or participated
- Event sales
- New customers

- Relationships started
- Relationships strengthened
- New things learned about customers, partners, business, and yourself
- Social media stats (likes, shares, comments, new followers, etc.)
- Customer reviews and feedback (written or verbal)
- Reviews and feedback from partners, vendors, helpers and volunteers (written or verbal)
- Things to do better (watch how this list shrinks or evolves over time!)

Return On Investment (ROI)

If you have hosted events or participated in shared promotions such as street fairs in the past, take the time to chart your ROI from previous years. Look at your goals and assess what worked best in reaching them. Things to look at include:

- Time (good time/hard time?)
- Partnerships (long-term relationships?)
- Money (total investment– expenses = profits)
- Numbers of people (new faces/regular customers?)
- Sales numbers (total sales/return sales?)
- Average sale (amount increase/decrease)
- Analytics (website and social media reports)

FAST START: Experience Marketing ROI Exercise

Take a stab at this exercise to realize the diversity of benefits that an Experience Marketing event could provide. Consider all ROI and think about community outcomes you may have realized: How many people helped or participated? Were they happy about their part? What were the shared customer benefits, earned media or other outcomes, if any?

Make a list of different marketing campaigns you have attempted in your business, for example:

- Advertisements in local newspaper
- Buy one, get one free (BOGO)
- In-store promotional discount
- Percent-off coupons in mass-marketed online services
- Grand opening or open house
- Fundraiser for a non-profit cause

Experience Marketing is a cumulative strategy that builds over time. To track your progress, your final ROI may be calculated based on all of your goals, not just the monetary ones. That's why it's important, when evaluating an Experience Marketing event, to take *all* goals into account—human, relational, networking, brand recognition and reputation, as well as sales. Recognizing that all of these returns are important for reaping long-term benefits will set you apart from others and strengthen your business over time.

Climate awareness

Experience Marketing events, as shown here, will not only produce the kind of experience your target market will love; they will lead you toward that long-lasting sustainable business of your dreams. Sustainability-oriented small businesses are now focusing on the triple bottom line of People, Planet and Profit. This approach is evolving into a more holistic view, combining goals for enhanced social capital, a balanced ecological impact, and improved financial returns.

Even if your customers aren't focused on climate awareness, you should be. Being eco-conscious will save you money besides benefiting the long-term health of your environment. It can also be a marketing angle in your advertising that brings in more people. As this new global awareness grows, you will do well to grow with it, both in your actions and as part of your brand awareness. Here are some tips for improving your environmental footprint.

- Cut down on the amount of waste by renting equipment when possible. Rent serveware like plates and glasses, or rent a barbecue instead of purchasing for your one event.
- Reuse or rent decorations.
- Discourage single-use plastic bottles by providing water dispensers. Use paper instead of plastic straws.
- Use edible flatware and compostable containers.
- Encourage patrons to arrive by foot, bicycle, public transit or carpool. Reducing the number of cars will keep neighbors happy and help ensure that those who must drive will be able to find a parking space.
- Staff recycling areas so attendees can learn best recycling practices.
- Generate electricity for entertainment with stationary bikes that audience members pedal during performances.

> **PARTNER OPP:** Partner with neighboring restaurants and cafés by asking them to lend plates, glasses and serveware in return for promotion.

Executing vision

Even if your theme is "Dystopian Junkyard," avoid old, uneven, or mislabeled products and services. Sloppy planning appears at all stages. Commit to perfecting a small event before gambling your reputation on one that you're not prepared to do right. Experience Marketing events require attention to detail.

- Better an intimate gathering among trusted patrons for your first test run than a big party that only gets half set up due to unexpected, unplanned, but avoidable circumstances.
- Better to hire someone or recruit a trusted volunteer and partners to handle things outside of your skill set. Don't end up standing in front of a crowd at an otherwise successful event and botch the names and introductions of the people who helped make it possible.
- Better to take six months to plan and prepare for your first event and get all the details right, than to throw one together in a month and see what happens.

Reputation

Experience Marketing events, done well, will gain a positive reputation, just like your business. Decide in advance how high a bar you want to set. Keep in mind that it's easier to start small and grow than to start big and have to scale back. Every element you plan, or forget to plan, will set the tone of your reputation from inception to execution.

You will see the highest, most consistent ROI when you *tell people what to expect and then give it to them.* Only go above and beyond that promise if you're positive you can pull it off. Being reliably consistent, instead of randomly alternating between genius and chaos, will produce greater cumulative results in the long run.

Costs affect quality. Determine the level of quality that you can afford before you are locked in to any contract. Be transparent when renting equipment. If you can't afford the highest quality, then lean into and celebrate what you can do.

Another best practice for Experience Marketing event planners is to be calm, straightforward and considerate when issues inevitably arise. The public knows stuff happens and no one expects perfection. The most spectacular events you've seen and heard of have had a million little things go wrong. The few that you'll ever hear about are handled so well that patrons feel like a part of the "inner circle" when they are compensated for the error. Bottom line, it's how you deal with the unavoidable that gains you the trust of those attending and establishes a positive reputation. A high-quality reputation isn't expensive; it's attained mostly through self-awareness and integrity, which shows up in many ways.

Reputation musts:
- Set up for event when scheduled.
- Start when promised.
- Clearly communicate expectations for attendees and participants.
- Follow the agenda you advertise as closely as possible.
- Maintain an attitude of collaboration and service.
- Deliver promised activities, contests, prizes and rewards.
- Keep areas clean and tidy the whole time.
- End on time.
- Clean up completely and in a timely manner.

> **FAST START:** An Italian restaurant wants to "go big" for Valentines with a "Night in Venice," but the only extra rental tables they can afford are crummy looking. They can either cover tables with expensive cloths and go way over budget, or change the theme, opting to "dress down" the entire restaurant to an equally romantic "Lady and The Tramp" night.

Communication is the entire foundation of your brand's effectiveness. No reputation, good or bad, exists without this most basic level of trust founded in quality communication. You must limit surprises, unless they are a natural extension of your theme and entertainment. Be open to and prepared for unavoidable or emergency changes. Stop rumors at their source and, where possible, correct the material or person that started them. Address concerns head on, as avoiding them only tells people you are either hiding something, or you are unprepared or out of your depth. Avoid over complicating or over saturating your customers with novel information that consumes their time without providing a clear-cut value. It helps to stick to one new thing.

Communication is strongest when it gets to the point quickly and stays on topic with a laser-like focus. Less is more, so distill information down to the basics. People appreciate concise communications that demonstrate a respect for their time as long as they are still understandable. There is a difference between a post-it note on the register with an arrow pointing to the bathroom and multiple, easy-to-read signs that direct people to the bathroom without having to ask.

Build trust by communicating solutions to customers as needed to resolve issues that arise. Mistakes won't look like a loss of control or insufficient preparation when you take immediate steps to compensate for them. Amusement parks deal with unexpected ride closure, a potential reputation buster, by having "front of the line" passes ready to hand out the moment a ride is shut down. Are people still disappointed? Yes, but nothing turns that feeling around like hearing you didn't waste precious time in a line that went nowhere. It's even better for the people that have only been in line for a few minutes. Who wouldn't race to the next activity with confidence after that?

Consistency: Differing times, dates or other logistical information on marketing materials can kill an event before it starts. Inconsistent messaging confuses people, compromises trust, and will eventually erode your reputation as a business that knows what it's doing to one that is making it up as it goes along. Start with the most basic, but pertinent, information and build on it to add excitement. The core information—what, where and when—is the lighthouse from which all the other tantalizing bits of light originate.

Just like your brand, your core event information must also be presented consistently. Size changes can't always be helped; but font, format, location and color can be controlled. You want a reader's eye to go to the same place to find the date, time, or location.

Consistency is also about ease. You want people to feel like they can rely on you for the long haul, and finding a new source for what you provide is too much trouble. This feeling develops through familiarity and habit; two things you'll never be able to establish without consistency. This is also why larger companies are slow to change logos, websites, or other fundamental information sources. When they do make changes, they are either introduced so slowly and in such small increments that the average consumer never notices, or they are announced months in advance and include incentives for customers to change with them.

> **FAST START:** Maintain a level of consistency so that your reputation is enough advertising. A brick-and-mortar store that keeps regular hours and carries what it advertises is consistent. A food truck that always parks on the same corner each Friday is consistent. An artist who posts new creations for sale at noon each Monday is consistent. Events that stay in the same location, start and end at the same time, and always feature the same or similar vendors and entertainment, is consistent.

Continuity: Avoid events, experience-oriented or otherwise, that are not in line with your brand, unless you have time and money to burn on extreme longshots. Well established businesses need to go slow when adding Experience Marketing techniques if they have never even decorated for a standard holiday. Continuity, from planning to execution, is the framework on which experience-based events are built for success. Example: While a vegan food truck might break even at a BBQ festival, a pit-master will have a lot of time to nap at a vegan festival, no matter how many awards they've won. Continuity means aligning your strengths within your field of expertise.

Design an event to be an extension of others or to fill a specific gap. A restaurant might partner with a nearby candy shop and bookstore to offer reading nooks where customers can enjoy their sweets and reading material. Look for ways to complement what is already happening in your neighborhood while marketing something new to your regulars. The expectations of your current customers must always be taken into consideration.

As long as your theme is clear, the senses are positively affected and announcements are well advertised and proficiently executed, a business can get as high a ROI on a casual mixer as they do on a big annual charity auction. Highly themed restaurants, like Cracker Barrel, or a bookshop arranged to feature a still-functional letter press, can be total escapist locations, every bit the equal of full theme parks. They can achieve this through total immersion in their daily brand as it relates to a theme. A Cracker Barrel is never going to throw a gothic-horror themed Halloween party and a bookshop where employees dress like book printers from the 1800s is not likely to host a Madonna-themed party. Why? Because dedication to continuity, as well as community, is a well-known secret of successful Experience Marketing events.

Partners can enrich an event and attract diversity by bringing activities, services, and decor.

CHAPTER 4
Connecting to Partners and Building Community Relationships

Intrigue, distinguish and honor people to build lasting partnerships

Experience Marketing events are best managed by a masterful trio of technical, managerial and promotional professionals like those described in Michael Gerber's classic book, *E Myth*. The three work together to make the diverse parts coalesce in the best possible way.

Unfortunately, the ability to hire two other professionals doesn't exist for most small business owners, so you often have to do it all by yourself. Entrepreneurs tend to be isolated and don't ask for help because they don't want the work of delegating. (Oh no, not another employee!) We are restricted by what we understand, what we want to focus on and what we do well. Let's face it. There is comfort in doing the same thing over and over, because it's something we are good at.

The event you are planning may provide an incredible experience for your existing customers. It may also bring in new customers that will eventually increase sales and strengthen your business model. But if you aren't using events as a community-building opportunity, you're doing extra work and reaping only short-term rewards. This is why it's worth your while to consider bringing on partners to help you plan, market or produce a kick-ass Experience Marketing event.

Partnering is one of the secrets of Experience Marketing success. By engaging with your community, asking for help, creating partnerships and relying on the support of other participants, you will start to develop the long-term relationships critical to the success of your business. You already have de facto business relationships with your suppliers, professional service people, employees, even customers. Recruiting and refining these connections will expand your opportunity for profitability, and more importantly, help you feel successful in business. You will start to know where to turn when issues arise, and you'll have more choices of people to turn to for advice and support.

Experience Marketing events demand attention at specific times. If you look objectively, you will see that the only things standing between you and success are the things you're not good at—yet. The gap in your knowledge, or lack of time for learning, opens an opportunity for forming a new partnership and adding to your network of support. Collaborating with others who have different skill sets frees up your time to do what you do and do it better. Make the development of these partnering opportunities one of your highest priorities. Be inventive in finding ways to entice friends, associates and relations. Offering them an opportunity to share their expertise may be the compliment they need to boost their spirits.

Look for partners who share the same audience

Think about the event's target market (TM) again. Are there are other businesses that might have the same TM? How about finding a partner from a field that you've admired, like a local scientist, sports pro or entertainer who might want to give back to their community? Seniors and retired folks love to be involved in fun community activities. Their energy level might be waning, but not their intelligence and enthusiasm. Elders often make great day-of-event volunteers because they've had a lifetime of experience dealing with other people.

You are probably already involved in trade clubs, business associations, service clubs or social groups that include others with similar interests. When you attend those gatherings, take note of who is good at speaking, who is connected to the local music and/or art scene, who is knowledgeable about food arrangements.

Get to know people involved in your local schools, churches, or elder facilities. Attend conferences, workshops, athletic or cultural activities related to your target market. Look up groups that cater to pets, teens, parents or veterans. Any connections you make could potentially lead to new partnerships in a future Experience Marketing event, as well as new customers or clients, if they fit within your target market.

You may already be a partner in conventional holiday celebrations or campaigns organized by community groups in your neighborhood. If not, see if you can find a niche for yourself in annual street fairs, holiday promotions, or ongoing activities staged by schools, clubs, business or neighborhood associations and other nonprofits.

Stretch yourself. Consider business people who have nothing to do with you or your type of business as potential partners. Ask an ophthalmologist, though you have never needed glasses. Partner with a realtor, even though you have no plans to move. Approach the owner of a pet store you've never visited because you don't have a pet. The options are endless. Seek owners of businesses whose customers might have something in common with yours, in terms of demographics like age, ethnicity, employment, or home ownership, would be good partners.

Even if you don't like to socialize, people are all around. Google by location to find a particular type of business near you. Take the time to stop in and meet the owner or manager. Hosting an Experience Marketing event provides you the reason to get to know potential partners and offers them the kind of public exposure that could lead to new customers. They may become your best marketing associates later.

Partners make hosting easier by sharing the load, but they can also enrich events with a diversity of opinions, ideas and resources. Partner roles can range from traditional sponsorships involving cash or in-kind donations, to volunteering for hands-on activities. Their involvement can free you up to focus on what you do best.

When interacting with new or potential partners, it is key to gain an understanding of what attracted them in the first place, and to honor their initial reason for joining forces.

> **PARTNER OPP:** When scaling up events that are best promoted by television, radio and print coverage, consider partnering with a larger business that has a PR department or contracted PR firm.

Developing a cadre of partners will put you on track to build a sustainable, supportive community. You will be strengthening your own business by gathering this community around you. Building community happens over time. You get to know people by working with them, relating to them in different ways, and offering the opportunity to experience a little joy together, one event at a time. Experience Marketing events can be the beginning of a mutually beneficial relationship that will help build a community around both of your businesses.

FAST START: Partnership Exercise in 3 Parts

Part 1: **List the types of partners you wish you could have on your ideal Experience Marketing team.** Some examples include vendors (flowers, catering, entertainment, valet service); professional services (insurance, legal aid, health care); social media marketers; and people managers (volunteer coordinator, booking agent, bartender).

Part 2: **Make a list of potential partners.** Who would be fun to work with a few hours a week, for the next few weeks? List ideal people you know (or want to know) from these groups:

- Friends, family members, employees and suppliers
- Service professionals (banker, insurance provider, utility owners, media reps, florist, nearby bar or restaurant owners)
- Neighboring retail business owners (especially if you don't know them)
- Local Chamber, trade group, or business association
- Professional planners, rental companies, theater groups
- Local government economic development agencies or officials (elected or hired)
- Community colleges, trade schools, universities, or large corporations' online job boards and service directories

Part 3: **Now combine your two lists.** Highlight the people who have the potential of meeting your pre-determined needs for money or time. If you hope to enlist a florist, you might start by selecting your top three out of those you know, plus any nearby. Choose your top three potential partners from the list you generated in Part 2. Strengthen existing partnerships or foster new ones by inviting these people to participate in your next promotion or at the very least to join you for a cup of coffee.

Promoting Experience Marketing events continues all the way to your front door.

CHAPTER 5
Promoting Events and Your Brand with Stimulating, Experiential Style

Experience Marketing event promotion keeps a laser-like focus on "selling the experience." Advertising creates lasting impressions with visuals and words that stimulate an enjoyable sensory reaction. Everything your customer reads, watches, hears or learns about should bolster their confidence in your ability to deliver the feelings and experience you promise. Convince them with sights, sounds and textures that they will be immersed in an exciting experience that has the potential to create new memories and traditions.

Marketing can be the most intense part of preparing for your Experience Marketing event. For that reason, you want to avoid unnecessary duplication of efforts and begin with what you're already doing to market your business.

Answer the following four questions in as much detail as possible for an honest inventory of your marketing strategy. Note both your strengths and weaknesses in your responses and add any new ideas that arise in the process of answering the questions.

MARKETING STRATEGY: TAKING INVENTORY

Ongoing Marketing

- How are you currently marketing your business on a daily basis? Give examples of current marketing efforts, both at your physical location (e.g., window displays, street signs, banners) and online (e.g., website with or without online sales; social media marketing through Facebook, Instagram, YouTube and others; sales through Squarespace, Amazon, Etsy, eBay, or others; direct mail or email marketing).
- Do you try to get more sales or referrals by offering discounts, sale prices and special offers?
- What is your current ROI for each strategy?

Event Marketing

- What kind of events do you participate in? (Chambers or Main Street organizations, other businesses, schools, local nonprofits, or others)
- How do you invest in local events? Through cash or in-kind sponsorships, hosting activities, sharing advertising, or other?
- How often do you participate?
- What is your usual ROI from this kind of involvement?

Advertising

- Do you invest in advertising campaigns? How often?
- Which of the following are part of your advertising strategy? Print advertising in magazines, newsletters or local papers; printed fliers, coupons, mailers; paid online advertising via Google, Facebook, Nextdoor, or other; sponsorship ads on other websites; seller platform ads on YouTube, Amazon, Etsy, or eBay.
- What is your ROI on each strategy?

Social Media

- Do you have a Social Media plan or goals for engagement?
- Which platforms do you use? Facebook, Instagram, Pinterest, Twitter, Tumblr, Nextdoor, or other? How frequently do you post?
- Are you active on LinkedIn, Alignable, or other virtual business-to-business networks?
- Do you know what your ROI is from each platform?

Marketing is a massive industry for obvious reasons. Considering any one of these sections may be eye opening. One goal of this inventory is to show how many marketing tools exist to help you nail your goals. Completing the inventory will generate a list of ways to keep expanding your business. Ultimately, the ideal marketing approach for your business is determined by your business industry type and target market.

TARGET MARKET

Okay, so you're ready to plan an Experience Marketing event. The process of planning an Experience Marketing event gets you hyper-focused on considering your target market and how best to stimulate their senses to create memorable experiences for them.

If you haven't identified your target market, also known as target audience, you will have a hard time choosing appropriate experiential details. If you were throwing a housewarming party for your friends, you would know exactly who was coming and what they like. Enticing strangers off the street is an entirely different proposition. You will be making an informed guess of how they think, act and make decisions. Get to know what your target market thinks and feels and how to stimulate their interests. If you have been in business for a while, start with the customer base you have already built.

Maybe your goal is to capture a new target market. You still need to have a good idea what they like to listen to, eat and watch. Do they care about pets, kids or elders? Do they have leisure time, scheduled personal care time, or can they only snatch 15-20 minutes here and there? The more you know, the better you will be at marketing your event.

Primary customer demographics (basics)

You'll spend less time and money by catering to the tastes and promoting only to the people most likely to attend your event. Research your target market and the most effective way to reach them at the lowest cost. Many online services exist to help you do this kind of research without leaving your desk, including Main Street, Business Association and Chamber membership organizations.

If businesses on your street or in your area are already having regular events, watch how effective they are and consider copying them as a starting framework. Try to find examples of businesses that are also of similar size and scope as yours. If possible, get help from a Small Business Development Center, the SBA, or a local Chamber, to school yourself on business basics. You may want to hire a marketing consultant to help define your target market more clearly.

Basic customer information is just a starting point. The more details you can gather about your target audience, the better you will be able to deliver what they want, enabling you to create a high-level business relationship. Defining characteristics can include any or all of the following:

- **Behavior:** Shops, learns, recreates, relaxes, works, worships (or doesn't)
- **Entertainment preferences:** Movies, music (include what they listened to in high school), live concerts/festivals, TV shows, theater, sports, politics, books, games, habits, hobbies
- **Favorite consumables**: Salty or sweet foods, alcoholic or non-alcoholic beverages, adventurous or traditional tastes
- **Economic, family and lifestyle**: Income bracket, house/apartment, own/rent, single/married, with/without children, pets/no pets, throw or attend parties
- **Social/cultural factors:** City, country, island, or traveler, family heritage (lineage like African, Irish, Indigenous, Brazilian), old or young, BIPOC, LGBTQ+

Don't stop with your customers. You will benefit from knowing more about potential collaborators as well, by defining the demographics of possible partners, groups, and other businesses in your area.

Partner demographics (advanced)

- National chain or local business
- Distance from your business
- Products sold
- Hours of operation
- Years in business
- Average customer profile
- Participation in local events and fairs
- Most common sales and promotional offerings
- Advertising practices
- Similarities between your businesses and your business goals

Marketing is wrapping paper

The best thing about promoting an Experience Marketing event is that most of the work is done in the planning phase. The choices you make in that phase are what you will communicate to your potential customers. So, once you have a plan, all that's left to do is to share it.

Think of your event as a handmade "group gift." The better you know the demographics of your group, i.e., your customer base or target market, the more specifically you can tailor that gift for them. Demographics, shopping habits and surveys will also inform your wrapping paper—that is, how you sell it. The promotional "wrapping" you use—online ads, fliers, email, etc.—needs to be thoughtfully chosen with your audience in mind. You want to excite them, but the gift wrapping shouldn't over sell or under sell the event. Don't market for a massive gala event and then deliver an intimate evening with friends. Don't market for a quiet summer picnic and deliver an epic BBQ with a professional fireworks show. Surprises are fine, but only on the level of what is promised. Don't let the wrapping paper outshine the gift you are delivering.

Below are two examples of a Customer Appreciation Day (CAD).

> **CAD Example 1:** You mail out personalized invitations containing professionally designed, embossed, golden tickets, promising drawings for amazing prizes drawn hourly. Customers expect prizes in the $50-$100 range, only to discover that you are merely giving away coupons, penny candy, and the rollout of a punch card that will earn them more discounts in the future. People walk away from your business irritated that their time was wasted and feeling that yours is just another business that over promises and under delivers. They tell others that you don't care about them.

> **CAD Example 2:** You mail and hand out a special flier inviting your existing customers to an event. It promises fun drawings for amazing prizes. Your flier gives example of a few exciting prizes but focuses more on the club that loyal customers are invited to join that day. Attendees discover that the promised prizes are exactly what the flier promised and are part of the rollout of an exclusive new VIP club with special discounts only for customers who attend events. Their membership will earn them more access to special events in the future. People walk away from your business feeling valued, happy, and a little excited to be a part of something their patronage helps sustain and build. They tell others that you're about more than sales; you're a business owner who makes an effort to connect with and listen to your customers.

In Example 1, the marketing "wrapping paper" completely oversold the "gift." Did the golden-ticket invitation make a big impression? Sure, but not the right impression. It set customers up for disappointment rather than preparing them for what was actually planned. Too often, businesses do this and wonder why their big splash only got them soaked. The over-sell is usually justified by this excuse, "I don't want to bug my customers, but I want them to know the event is a big deal. I prefer to go big once and risk rejection, instead of doing a lot of small stuff that may not work." They assign the same value to each smaller marketing action (like a generic flier), as they do to a big (golden ticket) marketing action.

The reality is people *are* busy—too busy to risk their time on the unknown. Don't risk a bad impression. Go wider with smaller, more affordable options. Advertise a single event with an email, a flier, a social media reminder, a mailer coupon, and a sign in front of your shop counting down the days. Using multiple (small) marketing strategies is not "bugging" a customer. It's your way of showing that you're consistent and trustworthy—a friend who shares what they know and love.

Experience Marketing events that are out of the ordinary are likely to bring in new customers that wouldn't normally visit your business. Just don't say something before determining that you can deliver on your promises. The same holds true for online promotions as well as brick-and-mortar store promotions.

MARKETING TOOLS

As long as your marketing efforts match and clearly set up the customer for the Experience Marketing event you're planning, you can employ multiple means of promotion. Here are some of the most common marketing tools available.

- Agents
- Banners
- Brochures
- Business cards
- Billboards
- Blogs
- Catalogs
- Contests
- Classified ads
- Charity events
- Cross promotions
- Door-to-door
- Door hangers
- Email
- Fliers
- Gift certificates
- GIveaways
- Newsletters
- Networking
- Online Ads
- Posters
- Postcards
- Referrals
- Signs
- Seminars
- Sweepstakes
- Special events
- Sponsorships
- Window display
- Word-of-mouth
- Website
- Yellow Pages

There are so many marketing tools, you can find entire books on the topic. Your goal is to use as many as you can to reach your specific target market within your budget, time and skills. Take special note of the elements you can duplicate. Be consistent, using the same design you have on a flier, on your sign, banner, classified ad or online promotion.

The reason to keep your marketing materials identical, or nearly identical, is to create or improve upon brand recognition. The more marketing tools or channels you use, the more openings for customers to discover your business, to be reminded, and to decide to attend. The tools you choose to use will reflect your brand and speak to the lifestyles and tastes of your target audience.

Branding

Your brand is recognized by its logo, name or theme, and has an assigned value based on the impact it has in people's lives. Experience Marketing works best when it is consistent with, or an extension of, your existing brand. If you have a country store, then the promotions you do will have a country feel to them. If you own an Italian café, your promotions must have an Italian flair. Your Experience Marketing events must not conflict with your core identity.

Your brand is a strength to rely on when event planning. For example, many businesses can host a Halloween party. But if you're a small print shop, you could throw a Haunted-Factory Halloween promo featuring your new "ghost-writing" service, free spooky postcards or posters designed by your in-house graphic designer, and a tour of your operation led by someone in costume, along with all the standard scary decorations, and fun edible treats like ghostly marshmallow truffles and white-chocolate dipped pretzel bones.

It pays to use professional graphic design services for distilling your brand into a logo. When new and still trying out visuals, start with something simple like the name of your business in a stylized font, possibly with the addition of one simple graphic or symbol. Images have the power to trigger different associations in people's minds, so choose carefully.

In our busy, over-stimulated world, people retain information better when it is consistent, simple, recognizable and relatable. For promotions, keep your message brief and easy to understand. Be consistent with color, graphics and event name. And don't forget to position the names and logos of anyone you partner with on marketing materials, as promised.

> PARTNER OPP: Share the light—and promotion—with partners. Use humility to increase your network mindset and work with partners or peers as equals, especially when they are in a better position to take the lead.

Three stages of event marketing

Once you have a clear picture of your brand's particular spin for an Experience Marketing event, your marketing strategy can be executed in three stages: the big announcement, ongoing advertising, and event signage.

Promoting Events and Your Brand with Stimulating, Experiential Style

Stage 1: The Big Announcement = Building Excitement

Once you've decided on an Experience Marketing event, celebrate it! When we have good news, we naturally want to share it with the people we know. Announcing your Experience Marketing event will feel like inviting people to a party, even if that party is a quiet meditation circle at midnight under a full moon. The point is, great announcements communicate excitement, one of the most infectious emotions we have. Excitement is the first experience you want to convey to customers, long before they step inside your door. Some of your best, most genuinely enthusiastic ideas for announcements will come in the first stages of planning, so be sure to write them all down. That excited energy is real and customers will feel it.

Once you have your basic event information in hand, the next step is to craft your invitation and choose the delivery systems you will use to broadcast it. Pull out your customer demographic information and outline an announcement with an eye toward drawing in and stimulating the interests of your target market or desired audience. Continue to use the same outline to keep your messaging consistent.

> **PRO TIP:** Free or low-cost design services are available from websites like Canva.com.

Your invitation must always include a "call to action." This can be as simple as asking people to attend, share, like, comment, or invite their friends. It can include a request to follow you on social media or join a group. Try offering an extra treat or discount if attendees bring a friend.

There are many ways to distribute announcements:

- **In-Person:** Hand out fliers to neighboring businesses, existing customers, friends, influencers and VIPs.

- **Direct Mail or Email:** Deliver announcements via USPS to select customers, or via email (using MailChimp, Constant Contact, Emma, Infusionsoft, etc.) to contacts who have opted in to your email list.

- **Social Media:** Promote your event on sites like Eventbrite, Meetup, Yelp, Facebook, Twitter, Nextdoor, Instagram, Google calendars, etc. Use hashtags strategically to help people find your event.

- **Video Announcements:** Post video shorts via Facebook LIVE Video (cannot be prerecorded), YouTube, Vimeo, Instagram Stories or TikTok, and embed on an event-specific webpage.

> **PRO TIP:** When making videos, add regular updates using embedded technology or hand-held signs, ideally pre-planned, to let people see the event coming together.

After mailing press releases or announcements, take the time to make calls to your local media, and if you haven't already, start developing relationships with them. Ask them to attend your event and to add it to their online calendar, if they have one. Post it on local event listing sites.

> **PRO TIP:** Having an embedded code that allows people to add your Experience Marketing event to their calendars with one click is SUPER IMPORTANT!

Stage 2: Ongoing Advertising = Growing Anticipation

Announcing your event can feel like scaling a marketing mountain, which is why too many businesses stop there. But why put all of your energy into producing one single blast of information? People need to see something many times before they make a decision about it. In her Buying Facilitation® model, Sharon Drew Morgan goes much deeper, explaining all the elements of change a person goes through in the process of making a decision. That's why it's important to use the time between your first big announcement and event day to build anticipation and help people decide to attend.

If you have a habit of starting big and not knowing where to go from there, use it to reverse engineer the campaign. Design the biggest and best ads first. Decide how many ads you want your customers to see up to three days before. Your first design is what you will use those last three days. For the rest of your ads, you will create a pared-down version of your original design for as many times as you intend to post it.

> **FAST START:** Replicate the invitation on the following page—a perfect example of all the elements an Experience Marketing event invitation should include.

Use full color photos that draw the eye and illustrate what the event offers so recipients can picture themselves there.

Feature your partnerships with like-minded businesses to create synergy and leverage customer bases.

Promote the venue, entertainment and/or service providers you have partnered with to keep costs in check.

Serve thematic refreshments including specialty drinks that invite imbibing. Providing a no-host bar reduces expenses while allowing for relaxation.

Make it easy to get there. Provide clear directions to venue location and include parking instructions. (Offer complimentary parking whenever possible.)

MOST IMPORTANT! Add a call to action. Enable reservations straight from the invitation. If your invitation is downloadable, check that the links remain live and clickable, or write out a shortened URL so guests can easily RSVP.

Offer an incentive for people to reserve early. The sooner you know how many people will attend, the more time you have to plan for them.

Entice guests with giveaways and prize offerings.

Bring in as many partners as possible and acknowledge them at every opportunity. More business involvement means broader customer outreach and reduced costs. Clarifying expectations for individual contributions and volunteer tasks will prevent any hard feelings and ensure maximum success!

Featured presenters can be a draw and make an experience memorable.

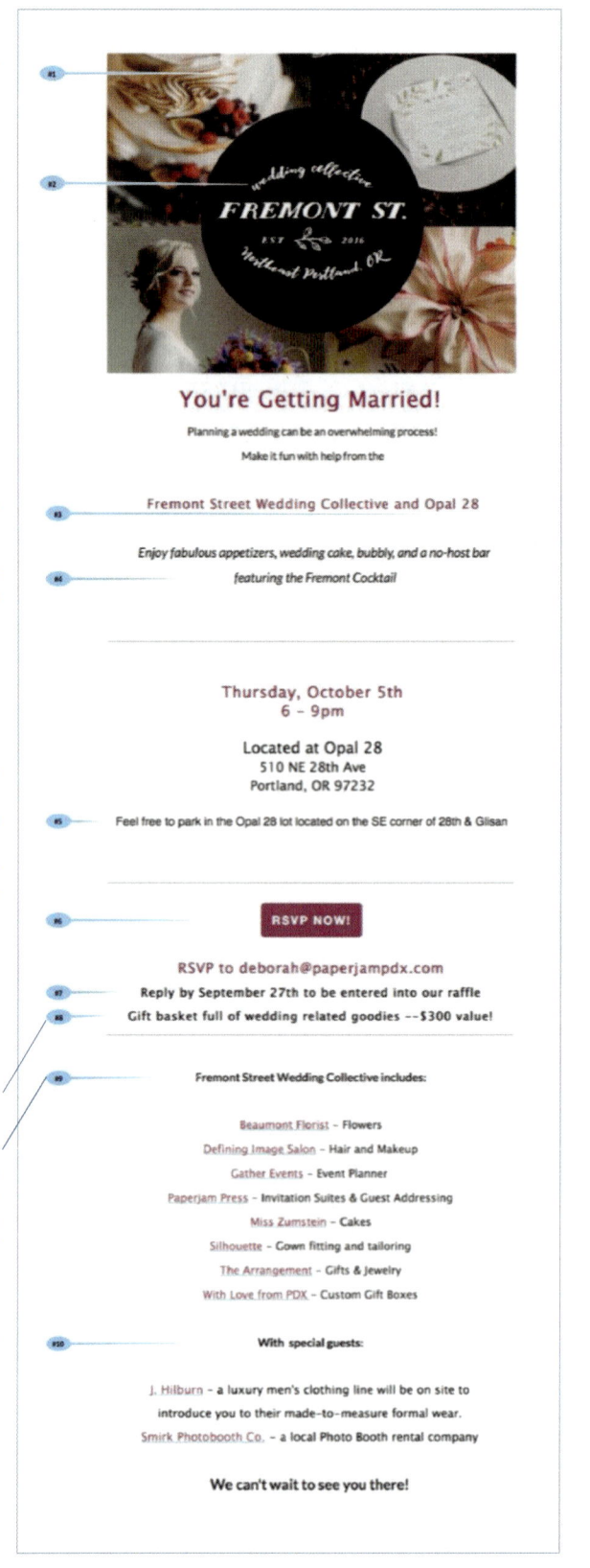

FREMONT ST.
wedding collective
EST 2016
Northeast Portland, OR

You're Getting Married!

Planning a wedding can be an overwhelming process!
Make it fun with help from the

Fremont Street Wedding Collective and Opal 28

Enjoy fabulous appetizers, wedding cake, bubbly, and a no-host bar featuring the Fremont Cocktail

---

Thursday, October 5th
6 – 9pm

Located at Opal 28
510 NE 28th Ave
Portland, OR 97232

Feel free to park in the Opal 28 lot located on the SE corner of 28th & Glisan

---

RSVP NOW!

RSVP to deborah@paperjampdx.com
Reply by September 27th to be entered into our raffle
Gift basket full of wedding related goodies --$300 value!

Fremont Street Wedding Collective includes:

Beaumont Florist – Flowers
Defining Image Salon – Hair and Makeup
Gather Events – Event Planner
Paperjam Press – Invitation Suites & Guest Addressing
Miss Zumstein – Cakes
Silhouette – Gown fitting and tailoring
The Arrangement – Gifts & Jewelry
With Love from PDX – Custom Gift Boxes

With special guests:

J. Hilburn – a luxury men's clothing line will be on site to introduce you to their made-to-measure formal wear.
Smirk Photobooth Co. – a local Photo Booth rental company

We can't wait to see you there!

SMALL BUSINESS EXPERIENCE MARKETING

Advertising campaign examples

Digital Ads: Let's say you're a pub throwing a Summer Tailgate Party where you will reveal your new partnership with a local brewery and kick off a VIP program for regular customers. You decide on 20 possible ad exposures for your target audience prior to the event.

1. Announcement of your Summer Tailgate party (date, time, location)
2. Announcement + reveal that there will be contests and prizes
3. Announcement + reveal classic vintage automobiles present
4. Announcement + celebrate a featured employee
5. Announcement + reveal special photo opportunities in vintage auto
6. Announcement + celebrate a vintage auto club partner
7. Announcement + reveal contest to find the picnic ant caricature
8. Announcement + celebrate a featured customer
9. Announcement + remind people to find the picnic ant caricature
10. Announcement + announce specialty foods for the day
11. Announcement + announce the employee favorite drink special
12. Announcement + reveal new brewery partner
13. Announcement + reveal a signature beverage newly added
14. Announcement + reveal musical entertainment scheduled
15. Announcement + reveal featured entertainer
16. Announcement + reveal VIP program for registered regular customers
17. Announcement + reveal full brewery menu
18. Announcement + reveal the door prizes and drawing times
19. All of the above
20. All of the above

That's 18 possible ways to get the word out based on one single announcement. You could do a countdown and reuse these marketing tools each day.

For this level of outreach, you will probably want to consider hiring a professional to design your first announcement. When contracting with a professional, verify that you will get ownership of image files, so you can adjust size and format as needed without having to pay to reformat for each use.

Notice that each subsequent ad confirms the basic details (date, time, location) while offering an additional reason to attend—one of many things that will combine to make the experience. Repeat ads build value and anticipation, especially when they include small tweaks that add information. If you're just getting started with digital marketing, begin with a goal of crafting 3-5 ads that build up to the total reveal. Run each for 3-5 days and then step up to the next ad reveal, up until event day.

Print Ads: Include a cute caricature or uncommon detail to draw attention to your ad, and a call to action inviting readers to clip and use for entry on event day. Offer guests who bring in a clipping free entry into a special drawing or a percentage off on purchases made that day. Adding such incentives to your ads is a small investment on your part, and the response rate can provide invaluable information for future marketing efforts. Try variations of this until you find the one that works best for you. *Train all staff well* so they know what to do when accepting customers' input. When customers appear in response to your advertising efforts, all staffpersons need to be prepared to collect contact information, ask customers how they heard about the promotion, note the date of ad publication and any other information that may be useful for future campaigns.

Plotting your event advertising campaign

Frequency: Can you advertise too much? Not really. Uninterested consumers will ignore you no matter what you do. Interested potential customers, even current VIP customers, will require more than one reason, or one info blast, to secure their attendance. People need reminders; they want reminders. *Giving them what they want builds trust.* Be smart and develop a campaign strategy that plots out frequency as well as distribution and placement of ongoing ad promotions.

Here are a few principles to guide you in designing a full ad campaign:

- Multiple ads are always better than one.
- Digital ads appear to offer more for less, but exposure can be random and is limited to those using the internet, so once again, it's important know your target market before investing.
- Have a way to track response rates for each ad, so you can improve on it in the future or drop it altogether and put your money elsewhere.
- Track social media views, likes and clicks with the analytic tools available.
- For traditional print ads, work with your sales reps to get a bulk discount and include a code or symbol to track results.
- Advertise a minimum of three weeks out, the weekend before, and at a key point during the week of the event.

Distribution and Placement: The event's target market demographics will be your primary source of information for the placement of ads, be they digital or in print. Traditional print ads often have pre-established markets and distribution channels. You'll want to place ads in locales your target audience frequents, or in the publications they are likely to read. Don't overlook local community newspapers and Main Street newsletters. Social media advertising offers a larger pool and more options for selecting a target audience. Pay close attention to the selections available and test to find the balance between too vague and too specific. Just like print ads, online ads can be run regularly and scheduled in advance. Search for "social media posting sites" and look for one that best fits your lifestyle and skill level. Scheduling services like HootSuite.com and Buffer.com can be great time savers, as they allow you to schedule to multiple accounts simultaneously.

> **PRO TIP:** To get a better idea of which marketing tools get you the best results, feature a different graphic element or coupon code so you can track what works and be ready to invest more in those that are particularly successful the next time.

It is not wise to invest 100% of your efforts in trying to reach an entirely new target market. Keep a minimum of a 70/30 split in your efforts, with 70% or more of your time, energy and ads directed towards the tried and true customers you're most likely to attract, and 30% directed toward a new, untested market. Being super consistent with your brand and themes is crucial for continuity of customer expectations and achieving the desired event-awareness saturation.

Stage 3: Signage = Controlled Experience

Stage 3 signage follows the same rule as Stage 2 ads: The closer the event, the more informative they become. A billboard along the freeway would feature one dynamic image, logo(s) and bare minimum details—what and when. The same goes for large posters and window displays. As the time draws near and customers close in on the event location, signage becomes your most powerful tool for designing the flow of information: directing attendees to what is happening, where to park, where to get last-minute tickets, a map, or a program for the day. Thinking through both outdoor and indoor signage can add to your success.

Outdoor Signs: Your place of business will likely appear different on event days. Thoughtful signage that is relevant, simple and highly visible will help orient attendees and give them a sense of what's happening. Outdoor signs are especially helpful for directing people to entrances and parking areas.

Outdoor signs are not an excuse to drop your brand or theme. Seeing your logo on event signs will alleviate attendees' uneasiness. More than that, external signs give the first hint

Make the most of neighborhood-wide events by expanding outdoor signage.

of the experience that awaits. The sooner you get customers into the mood you're setting, the more they will enjoy it. If your event has a Harry Potter theme, print signs on parchment-like paper and decorate with owls (stuffed or printed) watching over the parking lot. Post a sign for broom parking and directions to the Thestral stables. Ways of matching event information to theme can be as varied as your imagination.

Once you get the hang of Experience Marketing events, you'll find there are ways to reuse and recycle signs without compromising the integrity of your theme or brand. Creating signs with interchangeable elements or using magnet boards with large blank areas allows for fresh information to be featured on the same sign boards year after year.

Indoor Signs: Complete indoor signage will include directions to activities, maps to help people find their way around, and an itinerary. Indoor signs can feature partners and may include contests and entertainment. Ample signage gives customers the confidence to explore, not just get directions, and frees up your employees to focus on delivering the experience you've so carefully planned without having to answer the same questions over and over again. Including braille on signs within reach, where possible, will enhance the experience for any sight-impaired attendees.

Again, signs must be consistent with your theme; let no opportunity to stay on brand escape you. With the exception of safety signs indicating things like emergency exits, all other signs are opportunities to support your theme and enhance the experience.

Informational signs for customers include basic event information and:

- Descriptions and start times for performances, games, contests or other activities
- Locations of restrooms, coat room, bag check or additional amenities
- Food and drink ingredients placed near your refreshments
- Fees for activities and pricing for products and services
- Partner, sponsor, donor and volunteer acknowledgements

> **PRO TIP:** Make signs to encourage customers' self-expression. Dressing rooms can have erasable white boards, literally giving over the room to the shopper by putting her name on it.

Selfie station

A theme-appropriate selfie station is the most effective tool for generating in-house customer testimonials. Popular selfie stations offer customers a place to show off while demonstrating customer loyalty and a connection to your business. Decorate a designated area to communicate the feeling you want customers to convey. The best selfie stations inspire good feelings in customers and a reason to return, and they aren't exclusive to events.

Consider adding a station near your business entrance that can be dressed up to fit special themes. One great backdrop or prop gives people a reason to snap a picture and post it every time they visit. If you sell shaved ice or ice cream, feature a backdrop mural of a beach scene. If you sell books, have a giant book they can pose in front of or pretend to be reading. If you are a restaurant, enhance your waiting area with dynamic displays, demos, or hands-on activities related to your brand that your customers will want to share with friends.

The bigger the statement your backdrop makes, the more attention your selfie station will get. The more that statement connects with a customer's desire to be seen having a unique and enviable experience, the more it will get used. Where possible, selfie stations should be highly visible to foot traffic.

> **PRO TIP:** To get started, consider setting up a selfie station using high quality printed pop-up banners, fanciful signs, or life-size cardboard figures.

Promoting Events and Your Brand with Stimulating, Experiential Style

#Hashtags

Always ask your customers to share their pictures and provide them with the hashtags that will lead back to your business. Display hashtags in a prominent place, whether on a backdrop screen or a sign attached to the wall. In general, there are no rules for hashtags, but for best results, use 3–5 per event. Tags can incorporate location, season or festival, theme, special guests or partners and, of course, your business name. Examples are endless. To choose hashtags by popularity, watch the autofill suggestions that pop up as you type. Use the top three most popular tags that show up with the highest numbers. #LightFestival, #GreekFood, #ChristmasinJuly

Produce the events your customers want with easy activities and attention to detail.

CHAPTER 6
Coordinating Experience Marketing Events Like a Pro

Now you're ready to pull it all together. You've brainstormed and outlined the best possible event that will attract the kind of people you want to frequent your business. You've teased all out all the possible sensory elements and focused on the details that will excite and stimulate attendees. Interesting and supportive partners are assisting in areas that are not your thing. Promotions are in process, social media active and invitations extended. Last, and certainly not least, it's time to produce the event. The event production techniques and practical pointers offered in this chapter will help you organize and manage an event of any size.

Begin by making a schedule. A production schedule is a collection of information about activities, logistics and contacts, and a daily list of tasks with specific times and locations. Create one itemized list of *what* is going to happen, *when,* and *where* for the week prior, and then an hourly specific list for the day of the event. If there are more people involved than just you, include *who* is responsible for each arrangement. (*An event timeline, task list and production schedule are included in Examples at the end of this book.*)

> **PRO TIP:** A stress-free event begins weeks in advance, by thinking through the day of the event.

Order advertising, rentals and decorations online or by phone. Vendor agreements can be handled with short meetings (online or in-person) and almost all vendors offer delivery during business hours. Make appointments with start and end times. Stick to them. Media reps will come to your business and appreciate working with you through email, web portals and texts. When ordering online, study delivery windows and plan for delays. You'll never have a problem with early deliveries, but late ones could leave you and your staff stranded, scrambling and stressed.

Employees or partners can coordinate via web-based communication tools like Slack or Google Sheets that allow information to be categorized and updated in real time, or use popular apps that simplify sharing of lists, tasks and schedules. The more information responsible parties have, and the sooner they have it, the better you all will be equipped to solve problems before they arise.

Spread out tasks in a way that least disturbs your normal routine by preparing supply lists early, then adding extra items to your regular orders. Combine errands and pick up extra rental items early in the week or when making trips between home and work.

Entertainment

Schedule entertainment as far in advance as possible and get agreements in writing. Booking performers is a job often contracted to a professional when an event grows in size. Performers need to be informed of parking locations, load-in and load-out details, and the full schedule of the day's activities. Schedule at least an hour during setup for performers and bands to check sound and lighting. Save a parking spot for them to load and unload, and where possible have a space (called a "greenroom") for them to relax away from the action for the duration of their time off stage. Greet performers (or assign someone to do so) upon arrival. Offer drinks, refreshments and a storage place for their personal items, ideally in the greenroom you have prepared.

> **PARTNER OPP:** Ask a partner or volunteer to pick up or greet performers, even local ones, so they can easily find the correct location and get set up on time. For extra points, have this person serve as their liaison for the duration of their stay, so they have someone to turn to for any help, information, or supplies they may require.

Payments: Make payment arrangements for entertainment in advance. If paying by check, prepare your checks beforehand for distribution. Invite performers to sell their own merchandise to build goodwill. (This is good practice for any outside vendors who may be participating.)

Public Announcements: Introductions for entertainment, done right, elevate an experience and communicate professionalism to your customers. Write a script for any announcements or introductions that will be shared with your whole audience. It's important to publicly spotlight and thank all your partners, vendors and volunteers, either by name or by group, but it's difficult to remember the details in order to communicate them clearly with enthusiasm, so practice introductions at least once, preferably in front of other people. If public speaking is not your strength, ask a gregarious friend to broadcast introductions, or invite a local celebrity to be a Master of Ceremonies. Announcements can be a memorable facet of an event, so align the quality of your announcements and introductions with the experience you have created.

Set entertainers outside to draw crowds and stimulate good vibes.

Staging

Staging, the art of setting up, is the central point in the execution of an Experience Marketing event. It's vital that your vision is clearly articulated to staging crews. Follow these best practices to save time and coordinate effectively:

- Collect, inventory and store equipment and supplies in one location.
- Use the natural flow of your space to your advantage. Make entries and exits feel natural by adding lighting. Locate activities that need power or water where utilities are readily available and light them as needed.
- Use screens and signs to tell people what is going to happen and where. To reiterate, you can't have too many signs as long as they blend well.
- Clearly mark paths and alternative entrances for customers who face accessibility challenges. Keep access clear to activities, services and emergency exits.
- Leave plenty of room for your audience to relax, sit, stand, or even dance. Offer a quiet area, away from staged performances, where people can visit and hear each other talk. Crowding people can be okay, but only for a limited time (in post-COVID times, that is).
- Provide a general map that shows predetermined locations of food, vendor tables and entertainment, and pinpoints accessibility areas, exits and evacuation routes.
- Explain design plans clearly to anyone helping with setup. Visual mockups or diagrams are best. Even better, use pictures from a previous event (yours or others). Initial infrastructure setup done correctly the first time is a relief, and will empower your staging crew, whether paid or volunteer.
- In general, locate food and beverage displays opposite the entrance and farthest from your merchandise displays. Set up refreshment areas so servers can easily access them to replenish when needed.
- Similarly, live performances are best located far from the main entrance, to draw people deeper into the event experience.
- Kids' and pet areas are best when contained in some way, and set far from loud noise, high traffic, or other dangers. Set aside a quiet area where children and parents can cool out in case of overstimulation. If the event is pet friendly, provide water bowls and clearly mark areas where pets may relieve themselves.
- Set rental toilets so doors open to the side, not facing an entrance, high traffic area or stage.

Logistics

Anything that moves requires logistical support. This is where your production schedule will be crucial to your success. Assure volunteers and professional crews that their participation is valuable by listing *what* goes *where* and *when.* As a general rule, convenience goes out the window when event planning meets day-of staging. Whether an 8-foot table added to a crowded retail floor, or a 40-foot square tent in the parking lot, focus on large infrastructure items first.

Schedule rental crews at their earliest arrival time. Traffic delays, misread maps, stops for gas, multiple trips because a smaller truck was loaded on accident, equipment failure that leaves deliveries stranded—all these can happen and will, despite best laid plans. It's definitely worth the extra cost to post someone, ideally a manager or someone who fully knows all plans, to keep tabs on deliveries as they arrive, direct unloading, locate equipment, and recognize late, lost, or otherwise delayed deliveries.

Do as much as possible in the days leading up to and on the morning of an event. Portable outdoor toilets, for example, can be delivered the day before and padlocked until start time. Being 100% ready a few hours or even days early is preferable to being late or opening the doors with setup still in progress.

Informational signs direct customers plus offer a place to highlight event values.

Coordinating Experience Marketing Events Like a Pro

Setup

Event management requires a central information area. Even if your event is small, post a sign in your shop that identifies one place, table, or office as the designated headquarters (HQ), and schedule someone to be in charge of it at all times. This will be your Information Station or whatever you want to call it and will be one of the last places dismantled. Make it the go-to place to get supplies, connect to people involved, and check in and out for breaks. This can also be where vendors and entertainers collect their payments.

For larger events, the central HQ is where you, your coordinator, or manager will be stationed to provide information, updates and confirmations. A paid or volunteer manager is handy at this stage. They can be fully empowered to sign receipts and direct delivery traffic. Instruct suppliers to check in at this specified location before unloading. This will save you time if any last-minute changes have been made. After your HQ is in place, setup starts with the largest infrastructure items like stage, tent and toilets, then ends with the smallest details like signs and trash can placement.

Streamline with maps, lists and detailed instructions

Setup will be most efficient when you have these three things ready for your crew:

1. **Drop Map:** Shows delivery and pickup locations for supplies and equipment. (*See Examples at the end of this book.*)

2. **Drop List:** Details the items that are to be delivered to each location. Keep a master list and tape up duplicate copies at each location. Include a space for initials of the designated responsible party who is to sign for the delivery and account for each item. Drop Lists are invaluable references when it comes to correctly sorting rental items.

3. **Staging Packet:** Contains all the directions needed for volunteers, staff or vendors to complete setup to desired standards. Include a sequential list of tasks to be completed, from first to last, along with illustrations of the expected final result. An illustration can be a photo taken at a past event or a simple sketch showing how you want a table placed under a tent and beside a path, for example. Staging Packets allow people to maintain focus through multiple interruptions.

Additional setup considerations

- Locate garbage and recycling containers near food and beverage areas.
- Add an extra waste can near toilets and empty it on schedule to avoid overflows.
- Set generators or other noisy equipment as far from entertainment and conversation areas as possible.

- Stages usually require a sound tent or mixer in front of the stage; both require electricity.
- Sound and light equipment must be tested.
- Any activity involving water should be kept away from other activities, vendors, entertainment and exposed electric cords, and situated where water can drain.
- Place informational signs, programs and directions near entrances and exits.
- Decorate last, as appropriate to your theme.

Strike

Takedown is the reverse of setup. Literally, you can reverse the order of your setup lists and print them out with a "Take Down" header. Start with the smallest elements and work your way back up to the big ones. Remove decorations and signs, pick up trash and recycling, then take down large tents and infrastructure. Refer back to the Drop List when sorting rental items from stored inventory so they can be returned.

If activities end before the whole event is over, cover supplies or discreetly remove them to a staging location. Check ever-important equipment lists to confirm that loaned and rented items are returned to the right people or are safely stored for pickup at a later time as agreed. Make another pass to catch remaining trash and recycling. Lock up rental toilets and any staging areas holding equipment that will be picked up at a later time.

An often-overlooked phase is the cleanup that comes after taking down events. How you leave a space, even your personal shop, is about respect. We show people the level of respect we are looking for by demonstrating our respect for them and their spaces.

Inform participants, partners, vendors, staff and volunteers that the opportunity to work with you in the future will only be offered to those that meet or exceed this standard. The days of trashing hotels and conference centers as a statement of how "cool" you are long gone. Conscientious and responsible use is timeless.

> **PRO TIP:** Leave rented spaces as good or better than you found them.

Safety and accessibility

The creative aspect of Experience Marketing has the potential to pose challenges to basic safety. Don't let your theme override common sense. It could be fun to change your bathroom signs at a pirate themed party to Pirates or Wenches, but relabeling an emergency exit with a sign that says "this way to the long boats" will cause dangerous confusion if they need to be used (the exits, that is, not the long boats!). Clearly label all exits and entrances, as well as passageways that involve stairs or steps of any kind. Maintain accessibility for limited mobility customers, whether strollers or wheelchairs or motorized scooters. Watch for and prevent possible trip hazards. Be proactive about access and flow. Mark and walk paths personally to ensure attendees will be safe and the event manageable.

Be aware that some experiential elements have the potential of causing discomfort. Most people will self-manage, but Experience Marketing events may throw them for a loop. Let attendees know at entrances, or beforehand, about any specialty lighting, aroma, sounds, temperature, allergens, or any other aspect that could have a negative effect on their experience.

Safety Preparation: Double check your safety supplies. Here is a good safety checklist:

- Replenish first aid kits.
- Clearly label fire extinguishers and place in strategic locations.
- Illuminate signage in dark areas or when vision is limited.
- Leave space for people to walk around activities.
- Set bright construction cones or flagging to warn of potholes or uneven ground.
- Post event staff near areas that may be slippery or hazardous to navigate.
- Consider table or chair height for kids' events.
- Designate an area where children and parents can look for each other in case of separation.
- Leave extra open areas for anything involving pets or animals.

The larger the event, the more you will need to manage attendees' safety. Consult with security professionals and hire T-shirt security if needed. In some cases, it is advantageous to inform local police about event details in advance. In some cases—e.g., when streets are blocked, or amplified sound is planned—permits are required.

For emergency situations, conspicuous staff attire allows attendees to know who to trust. Set apart staff and volunteers visibly from crowds with bright-colored clothing, uniforms, vests, hats, battery lights, name tags, badges, or any combination of these. Stay on theme as much as possible.

> **FAST START:** A new retail store did a promotion for Holi, the Hindu Festival of Colours. Employees wore similar bright orange T-shirts and extremely colorful makeup, plus their usual name tags. This strategy kept the theme intact, featured the face-painting activity, and set them apart from customers with a single glance.

Money Handling: Many transactions have gone digital, but events often require collecting cash. To keep you, your employees and customers safe from theft:

- Keep money in locked registers, preferably in sight of video surveillance.
- Train cashiers in advance on how to handle cash transactions in crowds.
- Have the means to spot a counterfeit bill or only accept lower denominations.
- Remove large bills or make cash drops throughout the day.
- Schedule a safety supervisor to watch crowds at large events.
- Get tips from local police and notify them in advance if you expect a significant amount of cash to be exchanged.

Weather: Consider the time of year when planning any Experience Marketing event. Murphy's Law and the weather seem to have made a pact a long time ago to keep us on our toes. It doesn't matter if your event is going to be indoors or outdoors, weather will always be a factor in your preparations. That's why we always plan for the worst and *expect weather reports to be right.*

Here are a few ways to avoid weather related mishaps:

- Place carpets and mats for wet and muddy feet.
- Set food and rest areas in shaded areas or under tents to protect from heat and rain.
- Have backup water jugs in case fountains fail.
- Have extra tents, tarps, heaters, fans and/or ice on hand.
- Require outdoor displays, tents, etc. to be secured with weights or staked to the ground if not heavy enough to withstand strong winds.
- Consider having at least one backup generator for lighting in case of power failure. You may not be able to continue the event if the outages are prolonged, but at least guests will be able to depart safely after dark.

When in doubt about weather forecasts, make fun of them. Choose umbrellas, hats and other protective SWAG items, consistent with your theme. Try using cooling towels (kept in ice chests) and battery-operated fans (or the old-fashioned fold-up variety) in summer, offer hand warmers and blankets in winter. Specialty branded seasonal products can be profitable, as well as a marketing promotion. Some even become treasured collector's items. Adequately accounting for weather and being prepared for different conditions takes the worry out of event planning.

Partners in production expand event capacity and can lead to long-lasting, supportive friendships.

CHAPTER 7
Closing Thoughts

I hope this book has demonstrated the value and accessibility of Experience Marketing events for small businesses at every stage of growth. Hosting memorable events that offer immersive sensual experiences builds a community around your business while connecting you more deeply to your existing customer base. Growing your own business community through Experience Marketing will lead to long-term success.

This book has described all the steps entailed in planning, promoting and producing Experience Marketing events in collaboration with community partners. Combining proven event planning tools with the experiential techniques described, and developing meaningful partnerships in the process, will make your business more sustainable in the long run. You have learned the steps to better organize your time, tips on how to delegate and collaborate with others, and advice on when to hire professionals. The theme ideas listed in this book are just a beginning brainstorm. The number of possible themes is unlimited, and you will find the potential of promoting your business though events far reaching and powerful. Devote yourself to expanding your business community, and each Experience Marketing event will be better than the last.

May this book, and the Experience Marketing events it inspires, be the roadmap you have been searching for. Keep in mind that—like all maps—one must use the information within it to reach one's destination. Here's to the journey—and your continued success!

BRIDGET

BRIDGET BAYER works with organizations and small business owners who are planning to make their events memorable. She is eager to talk with you about how to turn your promotions into successful Experience Marketing events.

BAM • Business Association Management

Email: Bridget@BAMpdx.com

Website: bampdx.com

FB/Twitter: @Bampdx

Instagram: @bamstreetfairs

EXAMPLES

Event Management Tools

EVENT TIMELINE & TASK LIST

Essential for event planning, this is a detailed list of must-do tasks with deadlines.

DATE	PLAN
	Evaluate past events
	Decide goals
	Define Target Market
	Outline: Date, Time, Location
	Consider activities
	Draft promotions, advertising, & marketing plans
	Draft budget
	Add partner opportunities
	Identify music/entertainment
DATE	**PARTNER**
	Recruit partners to help or host an activity
	Invite elected officials & local celebrities
	Seek interest at local clubs/groups/associations meetings
	Recruit day of-event volunteers at neighborhood and community meetings
	Confirm partners' & volunteers' best communications methods
	Collect partner logos for online or print
	Solicit thank you gifts/extras for winners, performers (wine, gift certificates, etc.)
	Communicate day-of-event details
	Thank you cards sent out after event to partners & volunteers
	Types of partners, sponsors, volunteers
	Sponsors/Supporters
	Activity area hosts
	Greeters, Cashiers, Helpers
	Set up
	Clean up

EVENT TIMELINE & TASK LIST continued

DATE	PROMOTION
	Draft publicity plan (wish list)
	Update website (event page/post/calendar)
	Create social media event page(s)
	Collect performer bio info & pictures
	Write event announcement for media and send
	Post announcement info on web event calendars—link to website
	Create event postcard/poster/flyer/invitation/tickets (PFIT)
	Send PFIT to associations, local government, possible partners
	Order promotional materials (giveaways)
	Develop ads, newsletter articles, blog entries, radio spots
	Create promo video for YouTube, Vimeo, Instagram and/or Facebook
	Schedule morning media shows
	Email announcement to suppliers & partners to forward, share, like, text—include website link
	Submit event announcement to newspaper and media outlets
	Keep website updated weekly
	Social media event posts daily
	Signs
	Entertainment
	Directional signage: parking, entry, activities, washroom, entertainment, food
	Make outdoor banners & signage (for print)
	Activity signs
	Tasting menus (list kinds)
	Check-in & other volunteer signs
	Draft program script (introductions, thanks, announcements, closing)

DATE	PRODUCTION
	Activities
	Confirm costs (rentals, food, beverages, SWAG, professionals, fees, travel, etc.)
	Recruit/solicit performers
	Confirmation letter/remail regarding time, location, activity and setup/teardown info
	Rent/book sound technicians or sound system and necessary lighting
	Ensure power arrangements
	Confirm performer(s): schedule, equipment needs, contracts signed (if appropriate)
	Provide specific information to performers about arrival, setup/teardown times and locations
	Prepare checks for all performers
	Contests: Recruit and confirm contestants (web, email, texts)
	Recruit judges, participants, audience
	Create score sheets, game cards, notes
	Arrange cash box or collection mechanisms
	Describe awards presentation program
	Order/purchase prizes for activities needed
	Ensure promo items, awards, prizes, etc. are onsite
	Layout (draw) site map
	Secure permission to use shared common areas
	Check for required permits (property use, sound, street closure, fire, health)
	Temporary alcohol server (if necessary
	Insurance conformation (print out)
	Review security needs/plans
	Registration fees: Set up/enable online registration
	Reserve rentals: tents, toilets, tables, chairs, signs, staging, lights, sound, etc.
	Collect rental materials in secure location
	Garbage & recycling containers
	First aid kit & emergency contact information
	Production schedule—day-of-event timeline
DAY OF EVENT	
	Print production schedule & site map
	Meet partners/volunteers while setting up
	Review event duties with hosts, greeters & volunteers
	Decorate, hang partner banners, signs, etc.
	Hang sponsors, decorations, signage, etc.
	Close outside areas
	Label (sign) activity locations
	Set food, entertainment, rest areas, trash & recycling cans
	Set stanchions, fencing, tables, umbrellas, cooking & serving tools
	Stage/performance setup
	Sound check for performers
	Take photos at event—include partners, performers, volunteers & customers

Examples

TASTING EVENT PRODUCTION DROP MAP

Detailed layout of event activity locations including entrances, exits, toilets, food and drink, entertainment, cash registers and information stations.

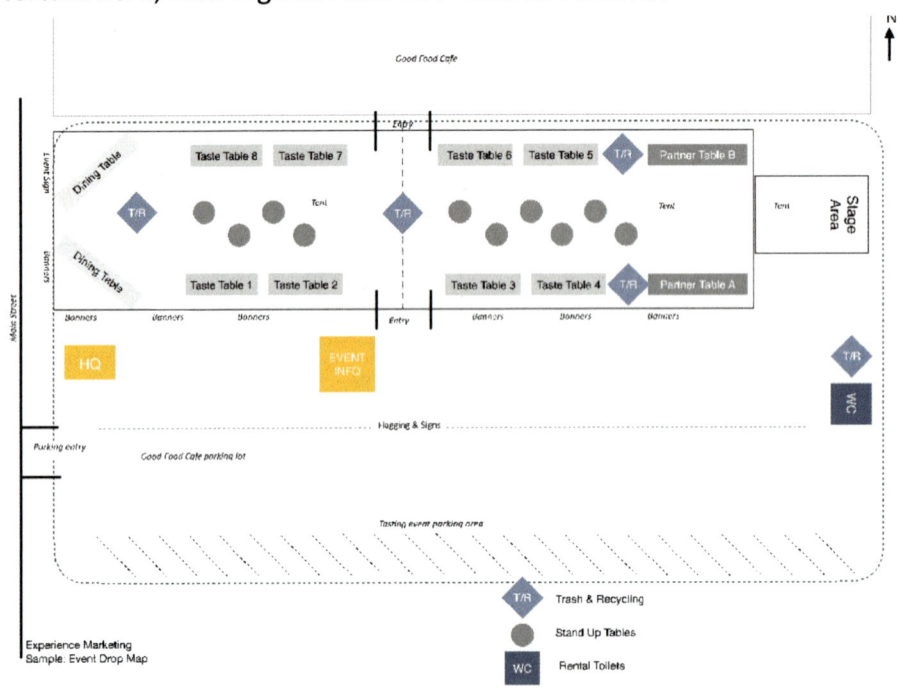

TASTING EVENT PRODUCTION SCHEDULE

The schedule of logistical details: what is going to happen, when, and who is responsible. Compile the information and make multiple copies to give to key volunteers, supervisors and anyone involved in planning or producing the event.

TASTING EVENT: Thursday, October 17 • START 4:00 PM – END 9:00 PM		
When	**Who**	**What**
Wed., 10/16		
4:30 pm	Event organizers	Meet at Good Food Cafe to assemble giveaway bags.
8:00 pm	Event organizers	Set out "No Parking" signs in alley and parking lot area to be closed.
Thurs., 10/17		
7-8 am	Toilet rental co. (WC)	Drop off toilet and hand-washing station in back of lot.
9:00 am	Event rentals staff	Drop off tents, tables & chairs at in parking lot.
9:30 am	Event rentals staff	Set up stage tent and stage.
10:00am	Event organizers	Close half parking lot. Add Tasting Event signs to barricades.
1:00 pm		Set up Information table at west end of parking lot. Set out trash/recycling containers throughout event site. Hang signs and decorations.
2:00–3:30pm	Taste event helpers	Help vendors and partners unload and set up.
3:30 pm	County health inspectors	Taste Event Vendor inspection
4:00 pm	**EVENT STARTS**	**Stage Music STARTS**
8:30 pm	Vendors (advised)	Begin breaking down
9:00 pm	**EVENT ENDS**	Help vendors load and clean up area. Stack rental equipment on corners.
9:30 pm	Event rentals staff	Take down tents and stages.
10:00 pm	Event organizers	Contain trash & recycling in full lot, sweep and lock rental toilet.
Fri., 10/18		
10:00 am	Cafe staff	Do final trash sweep. (Garbage service will pick up garbage & recycling.)
10:00 am	Toilet rental co.	Pick up toilet.

Examples

Made in the USA
Monee, IL
02 April 2021